THE CALL CAME ON A
SATURDAY
MORNING

THE CALL CAME ON A SATURDAY MORNING

REV. DR. JACQUES WESTON

The Call Came On A Saturday Morning

Printed in the United States of America.
ISBN-13: 979-8-218-414559
LCCN: 2024908478

The Weston Companies
Hot Springs, AR

TABLE OF CONTENTS

PART I
LIFE: SEMI NORMAL

The call came on a Saturday morning. It was at 10:40 and I was still sleeping. I looked at the phone and really hesitated to answer it, but I did. I made a mistake and should not have answered it, that call changed my life. The call came from my alleged partner, we had gotten in a bind from a previous deal and his uncle was allowing us to use his good credit to help us dig out of the hole that we had dug for ourselves. As Paul put it, we were in a foxhole back to back shooting our way out of the hole. I got deeper in the hole. I could elaborate about the partner later but I will tell you now. We were introduced by a mutual business associate. I was told that he was an ex pro football player and had a lot of important people he dealt with and I had no reason not to believe the people. I have no idea what he was told about me other then I was a minister. We met other the phone and spoke for about eight months before we met which was in Seattle, WA, the guy that introduced us was writing a REIT and Paul had people that could fund it and we were all going to get a nice start in business.

So we meet in Seattle and I notice he has not checked into the hotel yet, come to find out he was waiting on me to check in. Our meeting was that Monday and the offices were beautiful that we met in. Now he had people in the city yet we had to take a cab ride to the meeting, it cost $60.00 and by now we know who paid for it. After the meeting his friend took us back to his house to show it off, it was nice and then we went to the grocery store so that he could buy a turkey for his live in to prepare for Thanksgiving dinner.

We were going to stay a couple of days and relax and bask in luxury as Paul had promised but things came up, I left for back home that evening not sure how long Paul stayed. I got back home and was excited about the deal that was going to happen. I took caution about my finances but through them to the wind, I had a little money and was making good money speaking when Paul asked for wam, (walking around money) it was not a problem to send it and I never said no. Now this was my fault and it served me later as I should have been on my toes but never was. I have never applied the same scrutiny to others as has been applied to me and it's my fault.

I guess the writer of the REIT felt things were going to happen as well and he started calling me every day to ask Paul a question here and there and Paul started to become very irritable, please note I was the one in the middle. These two knew each other, but I went along because we were going to be rich and I had spent a lot of money already, so I had to see it through. One day things were getting tense and Paul got into it with the writer of the REIT, I was taken aback at first but just now I know what happened. A letter was sent to the investor by the writer of the REIT that put Paul in a bad light and the deal never happened. Paul got lost for about 4 months and of course I did not talk with the reit (real estate investment trust) writer any longer so I was just doing the same thing that I had been doing and that should have been good enough, but that was the problem, I got greedy and wanted a bit more, the thirst was all too real.

Well he calls me one night and really does not explain where he had been or why he had not taken my calls, I was glad to hear from him as he told me it was time to right the ship. He told me he had been working on a deal that was going to be great and 10 times better then the damn REIT. Paul's friend in Seattle was VP of a major telecom company and he was going to get a 100 million dollar contact with his company to install and monitor the GPS system in all of the companies trucks in the eastern part of the US and it was a three year contract, if we did good we would get another contract for the western half of the US, of course I was excited. Only this time I had an attorney in New York that I had come to know check things out.

He came back to me and was excited, he did most of the work at minimal cost and kept angling to get a part of the contract, I talked it over with Paul, he was an attorney, he was assembling all of the talent and he had even secured a million dollar line of credit, so he was brought in as an 20% owner. I was feeling pretty good about things and Paul had started to ask for money, which I sent. We had set the company up and everything was going good, we had technology partners, we had attorneys, we had banks in Dubai, we had a force of people.

Things really started to go well when we got the RFP, request for proposal from the company. It was sent directly to me and the contract administrator had called me on the phone to verify my email address I was going through the roof. I got a call from Paul at 2:00am and he told me not to bid the contract over a certain number, which I of course communicated to the attorney that was responding to the rfp (request for proposal). I delivered the message and we were clear on what it would come out at per unit and called Paul and related to him the agreement which he called his friend and told him and within hours we were given the ok to proceed and respond to the rfp(request for proposal) at the price we all agreed to.

The New York attorney responded to the rfp (request for proposal) and then he sent me a copy after it had been completed to, in retrospect I should have asked for a copy before presentation a hell of a lot earlier then 30 minutes before it was due. I had not but my thinking was that we all had something at stake here and we all said we wanted this thing to work, so who would dare get out of line or try to screw someone over. Now that was my thinking, I am learning everyday that everybody does not think like me, not my mother, my wife, my son, no one. So it was sent to me about 30 minutes before it was due, I would not have known what the hell I was looking at, I just ask if he stayed the course with the price we agreed, to which he replied, yes of course. I clicked send and we were going to all be very rich. I phoned the contract administrator and spoke with her, she told me the next step was an invite to New York to present our product and discuss contract perimeters. This was on a Friday and she said to expect a call the middle of the following week.

I went out looking at Bentleys that weekend and even put $5,000.00 down on one, I arranged travel and hotel for us and we were all set. I finally called her that Friday and asked how we were progressing, she told me that my company was no longer in contention and that I would get a letter from the company. I immediately phoned Paul to tell him and we got the New York attorney on the line for a three way. What came out of the conversation was that the attorney had been drinking at the Waldorf Astoria hotel and bragging about the contract with people and someone had told him that the bid was far too low. Paul got his friend on a different line and his friend had told him the bid came in too high.

Paul got back on the line with us and related the information that his friend had told him, for the second time Paul was cussing someone out and it was bad. The New York attorney, told him that we should negotiate this thing, it appears that he while he was in the bar talking he let out some names to people. Paul told him various unsavory things; I saw the car, all the money and the future of my family go down the drain, most of all I had gotten away from my relationship with God chasing this damn nightmare.

I owed plenty of money as I had borrowed from banks and individuals to make this thing work, I was mad as hell at the guy in New York but I had also let Paul down. We had worked hard on this thing and Paul really had not worked hard but he had contacts and now we had egg on the face and I had a boatload of bills as my income had dropped because I had all but abandoned my responsibilities at the church, I really screwed this one up. This is where the call came though on that Saturday morning, I was just getting my life back together and things were going pretty good, I fell again to the temptation of big money. Guess what Paul needed money; this call came 5 months after the last time we spoke.

He tells me that we really missed the boat but no hard feelings he had something that would get us out of debt and this time it was ministry related and should work out. He goes on to tell me that his ante has a white boyfriend that cannot stay away from her. He tells me that his "uncle" wants to help us out of our situation by allowing us to use his credit to get loans to start the trucking business and fix the building up they own down in Houston and the building would be donated to the ministry all I have to do is sign his uncle into the ministry board and of course himself. Overnight they became majority owner's f my ministry. If it had been a train coming at me I would not have noticed it coming full bore at me, much less say a word. I did not pinpoint the need I had to be a part of something. I knew I was going to do it and Paul kept telling me it was the best way out because we dropped the ball the last time around and it cost him a dear relationship. I don't know it to be true but I went along with it.

I did not do anything for about 4 months and Paul kept pestering me to get some credit cards and whatever I could, I was reluctant and that is when I went to the attorney in Little Rock, that has since stopped practicing and explained my situation to him he wrote u a power of attorney and told me that if they signed and notarized it no one could touch me. I put it in the mail to Paul and sure enough in a week's time it had been signed and notarized. We were in business. I got a couple of credit cards and a line of credit of $25,000.00 from the bank. Paul came to town and met the banker and got back home and ask the banker for financing for three trucks and a Tahoe for himself, which the banker gladly approved. I want to be clear, I ran the cards up as I was owed from all the previous dealings, make no bones about that. I used about $7,500. Of the line of credit for bills and did not care what happened. I got to wondering about the loan package because the banker asked for tax returns on the ministry, which I had not filed because you did not have to file a return for a nonprofit at this time.

We met for lunch and I was surprised and think it showed because while I was in his office before the lunch he gave me copies of three years tax returns that stated we made millions every year even years for which I had not been incorporated. I mean how dense was the bank, they had the papers of incorporation and it showed the company was incorporated in 2004 why in the world would you allow tax report for 2003 and further if we did not have to file why would you ask us for a tax return further still why would you not check with the secretary of state to see when in fact the company had been formed. I will tell you, the bank that we dealt with has had so many claims against them it's not funny.

No less than 5 executives of the bank have gone to prison for filing false companies and making bad loans to these false companies to cover the other loans made the executives run a damn pyramid scam on their own bank and other make loans, large size loans and have to sue the customer to get money back. The bank is built on a house of cards and it trickles down to the customers. The bank figures if it makes enough good loans it will cover for the bad loans it makes; therefore they take questionable loans it hopes of making it up and correcting themselves. They pay themselves high dollar salaries and get all the benefits and perks of the office yet the customers are the crooks. What a joke, I bet this bank turns it all around and makes it in the end, what a wonderful success story. I am not saying it was right to give false taxes r false information, period, but please do your due diligence.

Something that is very is that at Paul's trial, his defense he said that there was 8-9 other Paul .... In the Houston area and that they had the wrong one. Even the guy from the bank that met him and spoke with him testified that the man they had on the stand was not the same man that I brought into the bank to meet him. I will also tell you that Paul had written a check for $1,000.00 and the bank called me up telling me how I should not be writing checks that I did not have the money for and the whole lot. I went up to the bank and ask for a copy of the check or who the check was written to, it was Paul that had written the check and I called him from the bank, he explained to the bank that her had gotten accounts missed up and the bank paid the check and apologized to him for the inconvenience and even offered to apply overdraft protection to the account.

But never did they apologize to me as a matter of fact; they were the deciding factor in me taking the deal. See I was further indicted on a superseding indictment. 6 extra counts of bank fraud, this one was a no brainer and it contained nothing but lies, the bank said I opened a checking account with a different social security number. How in the world could that be the case when they had all of my information in front of them? My attorney and the prosecutor conspired to make me take the deal because I wanted to fight and I would have won or thought I would have won, it was becoming apparent that the information against me was slim. They indicted me again and the pieces fell into place, I took the deal of the one count It was a mistake to have accepted the plea, but hindsight is always 20-20.they did they not have video tape????

Furthermore, the government should have done something for me is the fact that I was the star witness, if not for me and my testimony, I have been told that Paul would walked gotten completely off and the thing is they found out at his trial that he was the one that did 90% of the wrong doing. Hell they did not have to treat me right just is fair. They were not, have not been nor are they. After I testified, I was taken back to the halfway house and about three hours later I got the message that he had been convicted on all counts.

I was told that if not for me he would have gotten off, not even a thank you for service; I did get a check though. I was also graciously greeted with a shot from the house director for having an authorized device on the premises. I know the FBI agent called and pleaded with him not to give me the shot, but the jackass did not relent, he was bound and determined to do something. I guess the name of a homosexual with latent tendencies of total gayness did not help my cause. When I got to the half way house I was mad and hell I was mad in prison if you want to know the truth, I was mad even before I went in. In mattered not it did not help me. My point I lost my focus and I paid for it. I must tell you, I would rather have stayed in prison then to go to the halfway house, now that is me, for someone else it most certainly will be a different story. I can and will tell you that I have changed and think I know better know and of course, when you know better you will do better.

Initially, I was shocked that the FBI came out to the house, they were looking for the home owner and I got it in my head that maybe they were not looking for me. They came back the next Friday and I realized then that I was in big trouble. I went to my attorney in Memphis and gave him the paperwork that I had pertaining to the eventual case. He told me that he made an appointment to sit down and talk with the FBI. He told me a day before that the meeting was cancelled and to sit tight. I have come to realize that he never made an appointment to sit with them, he lied. One day I was talking with his secretary and she told me you never talk to the cops and give them anything to build their case upon. About two months went by and he told me that the case was over that they did not want me they were after the co defendant. I was happy and relieved so I gave him $7,300.00 above what he had asked me for. I went on living my life and I did change the name of my ministry at the attorney's suggestion.

PART II
THE INDICTMENT

I was working and taking care of my family. We got home late on a Saturday night from having my son's birthday party at Chuck e Cheeses in Little Rock and I had a message from him to call ASAP. I thought nothing of it because the matter was over a year old and he told me it was over so I did not perceive it to be anything important. On Monday evening I got another call and it said it was urgent; I got a little panic in my step and voice. I called him and he told me to drop everything I was doing and get to his office as I had been indicted on 8 counts of fraud and was looking at some serious time.

This was on Monday and we made an appointment for the following Thursday, I was upset and worried and scared, I was going to jail. I was always raised with the fear that if the police came looking for you that it was for a reason and anybody knows that if the government has a case against you, they don't lose and it was for a reason, I was going to jail and I convinced myself of it. I got to his office and he had me wait what seemed like forever. My fear was further exacerbated by the fact that a marshal was walking around freely in his office and he kept looking at me, I thought that he set me up to be taken into custody right then. Well of course that did not happen but it lead to my paranoia and being scared it furthered the thought of jail and I knew no matter what I was going to try and make a deal with the government.

During the meeting he laid out the indicted and told me that partner had rolled over on me because the first one to the government that talks gets the prize so from the looks of things I was screwed. My mother was with me and she started to cry, he had no emotion or feeling for her. He told me that he had just lost his father and mine was nowhere near what he was going through so let's get ride the matter out. He told me he would work to keep me out of prison. I did not feel comforted. At the end of the meeting I ask about bail because I was being arraigned within the next two weeks and he told me to run and go find someone that could bail me out. What the guy did not tell me was that as a first time offense I would be let out "OR" my own recognicinse. That right there was the last nail in the coffin.

I met with the attorney in Little Rock that had been recommended to me on a Saturday and he was comforting to my mother not so much me. I went to the arraignment things went as the attorney told me they would go. What followed next was the $10,000.00 he asked for and I gave and he never had me sign a retainer. He never ask me if I did it, but he asked my wife did she think I did it, she told him I was a good man and anything I ever did was to support my family, nail in the coffin for him, at that point the movement of my case changed

It is August of 2007 and I sit in a court room, indicted on 8 counts of fraud. None of it true, but sitting there I knew I had no chance. 13 people were being arraigned that morning and some of them lengthy, the judge made me last. I found that he had just been appointed and the firm he came from was the one my former attorney wanted me to hire, I did not hire them and the judge as showing me that I was in for a rough ride. AT times during this process I had hope that I would walk away a free man but something always haughted me. Ws I guilty of this absolutely not, but I know that I had done things in the past and I had to pay for them.

I was always told you may not be guilty of what they got you for but there is something in your past. This rang true with me, nothing I was proud of but it was time to pay the piper. I just had hope that the system would be just I come away disillusioned that the system is not just, the very country that we live in the greatest country on earth is biased and prejudiced, that is what haunts me. In the natural there is no way that I should have gone to jail the charges should have been dropped and for this case my entire life is affected for the rest of my life is that fair, who can say but it is what it is.

What takes place over the next 10 years is the road of hard knocks and eye opening experiences that have formed the opinions I currently hold and none of them exactly favorable for the situation I encountered. I have grown from the experience and appreciate the fact that God relentlessly pursues those He loves, I am thankful, that He loves me.

I eventually hired the firm of an attorney that helped me in Little Rock and although he stopped practicing law he had a partner that was rated best criminal attorney in Little Rock for the past five years. He told me it was his job to keep me out of prison and he was going to do it. He told me that he knew people in the prosecutor's office and they did not want him to bow up at them. Fool that I am I believed him. I know now that my fear of the situation was driving my belief; n o man in his right mind would have believed the line this man was spewing.

I was indicted in July of 2007 and went to jail on June 1, 2009. I reported to Texarkana, TX FPC. The road I took to getting there was harrowing for. My attorney told me that if I pled to the one count of filing a false financial document I would be given a six month home detention sentence and allowed to resume my life. The prosecutor was in agreement with this. This pleading only after I was told that if I took a lie detector test and passed that they would drop the charges, this only after a document examiner told the attorney and prosecutor that she would love to come to court and testify that it was not me that signed the fraudulent documents.

This after, the attorney never did correct the pre sentence report that contained no less than 7 seven errors and which three attorneys told me that if it had been corrected I never would have gone to prison. I would have been sentenced at a lower point value and even as it was my going to prison was not mandatory, imagine if the pre sentence report had been corrected, I live with that. The attorney did not correct because he ask me for $15,000.00 two weeks before sentencing that I did not have. But please know that I did pay him the retainer he asks for in full.

Something interesting, we had a meeting with the prosecutor and secret service on Valentine's Day in 2008, the attorney told me how stupid I was for allowing this to happen to me and not to say a word because they would arrest me on the spot. During the meeting, I mentioned to the prosecutor that I liked his watch and he told me he liked my fountain pen. When we got out of the meeting the attorney cursed me out on no uncertain terms and called me every name in the book. He did this to beat me down and basically force a plea out of me.

I will mention that attorney Sam Peroni told me I was bullied into taking the plea and for a mere $25,000.00 he could have it reversed on appeal. Keep in mind; I did not have the $15,000.00 the first attorney had asked me for two weeks before sentencing where I to come up with it now was.

Trust is a strange thing I had absolutely no trust in the attorney. You don't speak to someone in the manner that he spoke to me. Looking back, he really did set me up for prison; I only hope that the best comes to him. He spoke to me in terms that no client should have to endure especially when you are paying someone he asked for the extra $15,000.00 because he knew that I could not pay it therefore it made it easier for him to sale me down the river. All too often people want to take a position of power in life and look down at others, why??? They suffer from low self esteem. Funny thing, I found out that the first attorney filed with the fed and got paid for representing me, as if I did not pay him. Which is not true, I paid him over $18,000.00 and still went to jail. I was sent to jail even though it was a first time offense, I had a cancer stricken mother and a young child and many letters of support for the work I had done within the community, the judge told me they were fake and told my mother at sentencing that she reminded him of an old Austrian song, the mother sees her child through rose colored glasses not the truth. The attorney had just had a case of a young woman with a small child that worked at a mortgage company he told me. Said that papers were flying back and forth and before she knew it, she was indicted for mortgage fraud. He had compassion on her because the baby's father had left her and who care for the baby if she went to prison? I left the same way about myself with my son and mother, who would care for them and I ask him that very same question, he replied, who gives a damn you made his problem and you should have thought about them before you did it. He had more than enough papers and intent to clear me but h did not see fit to. I say this because it is the truth not me being in denial.

On Valentine's Day in 2008 we met with the prosecutor and the secret service, my attorney told me not to say a word as I was dumb and he did not want to let the prosecutor know just how dumb I was. The prosecutor mentioned to me that he liked my fountain pen and I told him that I liked his watch. At meetings end, the attorney, cursed me out and told me I was going to jail because I was so stupid and could not follow directions. He told me I was going to jail. About three weeks later I got a call from my probation officer telling me that he understood that I was going to accept a plea bargain. I told him that it was news to me and within 10 minutes I got a call from my attorney that I had a big mouth and needed to keep it shut. I realized soon after that the attorney never had intended to fight for me and keep me out of prison. He continued to tell me I was a minister that had gone wrong and needed correction.

I did try to change attorneys but I had no money, I went back to the federal defender office without luck. The woman that called me told me after sentencing how disappointed she was in the matter, because she told me that she really could have helped me.

PART III
PRISON LIFE AT TEXARKANA, FCI

After all the legal wrangling I was set to go to jail, the judge allowed me to appeal the case even though I did plead. The new attorney told me that she would keep me out of prison until the sentence was overturned. I was to report June 1, 2009 to Texarkana FPC, but that was not going to happen I was told. So on that morning, I took my son to school, got breakfast for my mother and myself and went back to the hotel we were staying at. Now on Saturday the attorney told me I was not going to jail, at 9:45am the following Monday I got the call that I had to report by 1:00pm or face the U. S. marshal's who would be looking for me. My mother had to take me to prison.

The hardest thing I had to do in life was to watch my mother try to drive a vehicle she had never driven and worse yet to drive after not having driven in 4 years, in that time she had cancer, guillaume barre syndrome and was in no condition. I felt like a total failure walking into that prison yet at the same time I was not scared I was more relieved to be getting on with my life. The unknown bothered me but like I said my family had my concern. My first night in prison was filled with worry for my mother, my son and worry about me. However, in a strange twisted way I felt a great sense of relief that the trouble was all over. I think law enforcement purposefully keeps you hanging in the balance of troubles as a way of breaking you down and makes you eager to accept the fate you are going to be dealt.

I walked behind the fence and was processed into prison and I thought I was going to be behind the fence and had an image of a cell with really rough people so when the counselor told me to get in the van I was a little amazed. I was not going behind the fence but to the camp which essentially was a babysitting exercise for the staff. This cell or house as it was termed had no door to it, we were free to roam the yard and you could actually walk off the yard as it was a public soccer field and football field less than 200 yards away. Some guys had their wives and girl friends stand on the field and show their breasts and bend over to show them what they were missing. Some guys made regular runs from the prison to get high and buy alcohol and yes have sex.

Prison was and is a harsh place. You have guys that have been at the medium and low and have not transitioned their minds to being at a camp, but they use the fact that they have been behind the fence as a threat as it were of violence or to enhance their standing in prison. Let me tell you one thing right now, there no nobody at a camp looking for trouble, not a one. People talk bad but nobody is going to bust a grape, no one.

It took almost three from indictment to prison; I believe the government wears you down so that when the time comes for prison you are almost relived to be there, I know that I was. I had four cellmates or celli's as they call them. They were all white and repeatedly made me know that they had never been around a black guy before, so if we slip and say nigger we mean no harm. I will tell you that the first two-three weeks in prison is an exercise in boredom as what you do most are sleep; they are testing you medically and educationally. After you are cleared you have to find a job. Whites work on the farm or have higher grade positions at UNICOR, Mexicans work in the kitchen and control the flow of food at the camp and Blacks have the labor positions. It is funny but in a den of criminals racism still exists. I got a job as a tutor and taught GED to mostly Mexican and whites and some blacks.

It would surprise you to know that some people who look respectable and socially acceptable are really dumb and I think this is part of the racial problem in the world. Whites will always be accepted but I had grown men who had good jobs and owned their own businesses that I taught GED to, most never passed as they were not interested in doing so, they had something to go back to. Mexican's never made the translation and was forever lost in the classroom. Blacks rarely tried and were eager to go back to baking the pies and slinging the bags. I had one guy that was a trainer and had a near perfect body, he sold plenty of drugs in the world and when it came time to come to class, he would be allowed to sign his name and leave, he had no hope of ever passing anything and came to e many times to learn how to pronounce a word. It was tough being a GED teacher because most saw you as uppity and therefore you were alienated a lot but that was fine.

Everybody in prison has a hustle, from selling you shoes stolen from commissary, to selling you food from the kitchen to getting you better clothes and socks and underwear, everybody had a hustle. I caught onto this when my white celli starting making tamales every weekend and he was repaid with items from commissary, he kept his locker full and people look at what you buy and how full your locker is. Toward the last 6 months of my term I caught on with the hustle and started doing other guys DAP program paperwork. I did book reports, wrote letters for guys, typed up emails, filled out legal papers, my family only had to send me money for the phone. I wish that I had learned earlier in the game. A big part of prison is the store man, whatever you get you pay double, they perform a service but if you can stay away from them by all means do so.

I had all the fruit and leftover food I wanted when I started my hustle. I never sought anyone out; I let them come to me. I knew people were there for a reason so I never set a price I let them pay me what they thought was fair, many times I felt over paid but in reality, this was stuff they could not do on their own, I could have charged more but did not. My point, most of the guys I was in with was drug dealers and just because you are in prison, you never stop being who you are. Prison is nothing but a sub culture, the same stuff that goes on in the world goes on in prison.

We had a guy that was completing a 10 year bid and was a very smart guy, who had no high school diploma but could have been a professor, at any rate, he made it a practice to go to the motel once a week and had the latest tennis shoes. As a matter of fact when McDonalds introduced the line of Angus burgers and iced coffee's I wanted one badly. I slept in the fifth man bunk and right by the window and one night around midnight as I was writing a sermon, I heard the words, "Rev open the mutha..... window" I did and not to my surprise but to my delight I sat in the moon light eating a bacon cheese angus burger drinking a vanilla ice coffee, what a treat, I started having "real world" food once a week, it was expensive but worth it as the food in prison is no damn good. One of the Mexican guys I did work for and got him transferred closer to home worked in the kitchen, my work paid off with plenty of pop tarts and actual cakes what a dream, I laughed at the time because it was like I was getting away with something, but it was not funny it was tragic. It will surprise and sadden one to know just how low they can descend to.

What happens in prison is all systematic, the administration feels that the inhabitants have to be demoralized and controlled after all, they could not make it in the real world. So you have guards and counselors who mostly are ex military running the show. No offense to the military but the guards are taught not to question too much and just go by the book, and this is sad because the book really is no book yet a manual of threat and intimidation. The first thing you learn is that you can never win, this means throw common sense out of the window and do what this inept person says or you will be thrown in the whole and lose your chance at good time which of course everyone wants as they desire to get out of prison as soon as possible. The very system teaches you to lie, cheat do whatever needs to do done. My point if you try to be honest and do the right thing especially when working on a CO's crew they can get you fired for NO good reason. Now a lot of inmates say, forget him his wife did not give him any last night, well think about it, you are there with men who will not get any for years to come, no excuse for bad behavior.

There was a CO who ran a paint crew and by all standards was a plain idiot, his wife of no more than three months passed unexpectantly and he made a turn just as unexpectantly, saying that even though we were inmates we were human and should be treated as such, not quite human but with some level of manhood. He did not come as far as one would hope, but he was on the road. Another time, I was in class, the administration calls it programming, the class was Criminal thinking and the funny thing is, the prison system takes all of its course work from DAP (drug awareness program) and mainlines it for all inmates and strongly suggests you take classes.

A rumor is that the more programming you do the more time you will get off your sentence, big lie.

Nonetheless, a lot of inmates take programming. We are in class and the teacher tells us that we should have a better view of the CO's because they are people with jobs to do and are human. She went on to recount the issue going around the prison about the behavior of one CO and three or four inmates mentioned what he had done and the women had the nerve to tell us that the CO's wife had just taken him a good sum in divorce and he was very upset by it, my response to that, is silly, he had his freedom and the choice to do whatever he needs to do he does not deserve to take out his frustration on the inmates no matter what he is going through. This happens all too often.

One thing that really upset me was that a CO would claim the job they had and talk down to the inmates. One morning I was taking my laundry and because I did not have a job yet, I took my cellmates laundry as well. I never saw this as an issue. On Fridays you were able to get clean bedding so I dropped off mine and the cellmates and ask for two roll outs, now the inmate knew what I was doing, but the CO saw me getting two and he cursed me out for trying to get away with his sheets and threatened to kick my ass if he found me doing it again. He knew what I was doing because as a new inmate no way in the world are you going to get two sets of laundry, however he had to make a point of getting his bluff in. Conversely, the same inmate I took the laundry for called him by the first name and even drove his truck around the prison. Of course they were white; they get the best jobs in the system and make neither excuse nor apology for it.

I was having a very bad time in prison. I am not putting myself over anyone mind you but I was not use to the system. A lot of people that have been in prison have been there before and know how the system works. I had not been arrested before and was in over my head here. At any rate, I was having a bad day and here comes a rather large black guy giving me the eye; I thought we were going to have a fight. I was in over my head, I knew I was going to have a hard time here; he was 25 years younger, bigger and much stronger. What happened next blew my mind, I go up to him and ask what exactly is his problem and quickly retort, please stop I don't have that much time to hear them, he did not understand this comment, instead he reaches out and hugs me tells me he saw me preach at his church and whatever he can do for me while I was in prison, he would do. This incident went a long way in making my life easier in prison. It was also validation that God had not left me, I had been praying constantly for His help. Yu never know how God will come or how He will fix it, but He will.

I also find it interesting that the CO's would use the inmates only the white ones to do labor at their places of business and of course special privileges would come with it. I often ask myself this question, how do drugs, alcohol, tobacco get on campus? Now they check you when you have a visitor, they know what going on yet, they get all up in arms if and when one of their workers is too drunk to come to work or when they tobacco gets out of hand. I guess in a reverse they will let us be men as long as it does not get too out of control. My point, the CO's is the ones allowing and assisting the contraband to be brought into the prison and they act like they don't know a damn thing. Yet we are the criminals. Now it sounds as if I am complaining about the CO's and I am they are total hypocrites with a limited future. I say this after having McDonalds and Kentucky fried chicken brought to me for four months once a week.

I was glad to get out when I did because the prison is really a den of thieves and scammers. I remember a black guy had a job as a cook, well he would give out the smallest bits of food if it were chicken or ham or roast beef when you came through the line but after work, he would fly to his room and let the selling begin. Well he had his phone in his cooler and he had broken down the phone into three pieces and each fit into a portion of the cooler. Now the administration knew he had a phone but they said nothing. One day he was to give a Mexican some of the food out of the kitchen, if memory serves me it was someone's birthday or release day and he was throwing a party for the person, the black guy did not give the food to the Mexican, I think it was 5-10 pounds of ground beef. To no one's surprise, the next morning the CO's were at the black guys cell searching it for a phone, it took them less than two minutes they went right to it and put it together and turned it on, the guy's wife was calling at the same exact time, no joke. The guy ended up being sent elsewhere, his place in the kitchen was taken y a Mexican guy and the blacks suffered a loss in terms of food service.

Now if you want stories I got a lot of them but I am going to share a couple before I get back to my release and the twists and turns of our law enforcement brothers.

We had a guy that we called Uncle Keith, we did so because in everyone's family there is an uncle or cousin who just aint right, either thinking or acting. Now Keith was a truck driver by trade and a nice enough guy to be around. He had problems at home and had a cell phone to call whenever he needed to. He had gotten into an argument with his wife at his last visit and she had not put any money on his phone, so he kept calling his wife from the prison phones telling her that he needed her to put money on his cell phone so he could talk to her and tell her what to do with the latest shipment. On his way back to his cell, the IA (internal affairs/investigations) was there and we never saw Keith again, as he was being lead through the doors he kept hollering that he was going to name names, needless to say I went without Real world food for about two weeks.

One of the more noble positions in the prison system is the store man. You only go to him when you don't have something and you are really hungry. Most times your family or the person holding you down has missed a week and will catch up the following week, but the problem is that now you are in debt twice as much and your family only is sending you debt for the regular period which causes you to get your hustle on or do other things.

We had a store man and he controlled most of the flow of the store traffic on campus. I mean he was paying people to use their lockers to store food; he was going to rooms with three or four people and getting the spare lockers so that he could use them for food storage. He would cook for people on the weekend and he made cheese cakes like nobody's business. Well the problem was that he let a guy get into real debt with him, I mean about $100.00, not a lot on the street but when you are in prison it amounts to something. This guy that owed the store man worked in the kitchen and was his supply of fresh vegetables and meats when they were good food days.

The store man would cook for others on weekends and make good money from the guy that owed him. The guy would trade fresh food for commissary items from the store man and they worked well. However, the kitchen guy got some kind of rash or something and could not work, but he still maintained getting things from the store man. I heard him tell the store man that his family was sending the money and got various things. His other problem was that he was waiting for people to give him commissary to pay him for the food he had given them, it was not happening.

Well this is prison and people not only talk but they lie, a lot. Someone went to the store man and told him that he overheard the original guy talking about how he was not going to pay him and other things well the store man went to the guy and they get into it not fighting but causing a scene, a scene big enough to draw the attention of the CO on duty. The CO got the matte dealt with but the problem was that new it was in the log book and the day administration would take note of it and now the other people most of the ones that owed store man had written cop outs on store man. A cop out in pure form is meant to address some issue within the prison but convicts use them as tools to rat other guys out.

By the time the day CO's and counselors and case managers came in the box was full of cop outs and what did the day administration do they checked the locker of the store man and according to rules they found not he was not in compliance with certain food items and they found his list of people that owed him. What started next was he was in violation of this rue and that rule; he had too many pillows too many tee shirts. They wrote him series of shots, at the end o the day his level had gone up and he was no longer able to stay at the camp, he had to get transferred and put behind the fence. Now store man did not do anything wrong per se, but he did have a store and prison rues do not allow you to get anything from another prisoner.

Not only was store man transferred and now at a new security level he lost good time ensuring his stay in the bop to be extended, but he lost all the food he had in other lockers which I was told was about $2,500.00 worth and he lost the weekly tabs that people owed, me being one of them. My tab was about $6.00, I had gotten some noodles and a beef stick from him along with some cheese to make some spaghetti. The thing about this story is that it was not the guy that owed him the $100.00 it was a group of white and Mexican guys that not only did not want to pay him but they wanted to split his business up for themselves.

It was my misfortune to encounter a little black guy with an 8th grade education, yet he got 30 years on this bid as he had done state time previously. He worked in the warden's office and by all means and appearances was a snitch. For him to be younger than me he said he had 13 children, funny thing he was not 100 miles from home, yet he never had any visitors and he always hustled as he had very little money on his books.

Scotty as a body builder or at least worked out all the while in prison and it showed, he was a little guy and I think he had about a 24 inch waist. Funny thing, mama punk used to iron his clothes for free. I caught mama punk rubbing Scott's handles one morning and licking his lips at the thought or at the past remembering certain interludes the two shared. I never mentioned it to Scott or anyone else, it was none of my business and I left it at that, but Scott had other feelings. He worked to undermine me on every occasion possible, if he could chip away at my legitimacy then nothing I said would have any validity. I being new to prison and keeping my head below the level did not pay attention to a lot of things going on. Scott trained me as I was obese, I men I wore a 52 waisted pant; he had a lot to deal with.

I was actually showing great results and man I was feeling good about myself. But about every two-three weeks some crap would come down the pie and I would be blindsided by it, because I had not said anything about anybody. I was accosted by the Mexicans for someone saying I put a cop in the box, telling on who brought contraband into the prison. That was stupid, how anyone could have seen the writing on anything I allegedly put in the cop out box, furthermore, I never put anything in there. It was a lie. Another time the store man was said to have put it out that he did not want to do business with me, because I did not pay I went to the store man, he promised me he had not said it. Just another lie with a tale/tail on it. You cannot catch them, so you got to let them fly. I found out that the lies were being planted by Scott, he was my only friend in prison, as I did not take to too many people, so his lies would draw me closer to him and he would share the commissary that I gave him with the people that planted the lies, prison has all kinds of tricks.

Scott had asked me to have a worship service and I had to ask the chaplain for use of the chapel, the chaplain said yes, Scott got the warden to block it and said the warden investigated me and found out I was not a true minister funny thing the FBI investigated me and fund it to be true. One day I was in the unit and it was around 1:00pm, now the unit was quiet as most people were at work and I had finished class early, so I went down to ask Scott did he want to work out early, I got to his room and he slept on the bottom bunk and had spreads tucked into the top and had closed his bunk off from vision. I pulled the spread back thinking he was asleep, but he was jerking off, that was the start of our relationship coming to an end. Again said nothing, but it's not what he thought. After all the time he had it was a second natured thought that he would do so, but heck he tried to act like he as the most honest, wise, sensible man on campus and something like that was beneath him.

He got really bad with me and of course I stopped training with him. I started getting dogged by some of his minions and it got really bad one day. Guy named "X" came and got me out of bed at 6:00am and told me if I did not stand up for myself with one f the guys he was going to knock me out right on the spot and have mama punk rape me on the spot if I did not take care of my business. To make matters worse mama punk was holding him getting ready, I am sure it was an act but it put fear in me. He stayed in my room while I got dressed and told me to handle my business. I got on the weight pile; it was just the two of us and I start to curse him out and tell him to fight me. He just looks at me; now this guy is 6'6" and built like a brick house he was not taking me seriously, so I start to talk about his mom, his wife, and his stupid children, I picked up a 55 pound dumbbell and I am shaking it at him and cursing him out, he gets up and tells me Rev. you one crazy mfer and walks off. But my troubles ended that day, that exact day. X made me sand up for myself and I did, issue over. The rest of my time was a piece of cake, a nice big piece of chocolate cake. Here I was being played by a guy that could not read write, came to me to pronounce words.

I have always found this one to be difficult. We had a guy that sold oil leases for a company and at the end of the story he had sold over $20,000,000.00 in bad leases, not sure how he arrived at such a large figure but he got there. He was due to get out in two years and his mother was in real estate and he had started to use flash cards and everyday would take time to study the exam. He was quiet yet personable. Now his family lived a good distance away and he had a young child that he said he loved. So it seemed like things were coming together for him. He worked at Unicor and was somewhat of a supervisor, but really had been there longer then some others in that section. I did not work there and what I am about to share with you is what I was told so you can automatically disbelieve about 50%. He got into it with his roommate because he was going too fast and the roommate wanted him to slow down and take it easy.

One of the problems with the camp is that although it is a great deterrent for violence you still get people there who have been behind the fence and are used to doing things a certain way and they use that to get their way or to verbally bully you into getting their way. For instance, they will tell you I was behind the fence and I am not used to doing things this way, see behind the fence I would just stab you or me and my friends would beat the shit out of you.

I remember one day waiting for my mother to visit and my room was on the back side so I would walk to the front row rooms, across the hall to see if she was here yet. I was a GED teacher to one of the guys in the room and it was never a problem to walk into the room and look out the window, which on this day I was doing. ON my way out this guy is coming into the room, sees me waking out and starts talking to me until I get to me room and finally I ask him what his problem is he proceeds to tell me that he is from behind the fence and when he sees someone coming out of his room he gets upset because he knows they have planted something in there and he would rather just stab me. It took my roommate to let him know that I was not that kind of dude.

The thing was it was this same guy that worked with the real estate guy at Unicor that was complaining that he was working too fast. The real problem was that the guy worked out with a back guy and the new roommate did not like it. He wanted him to hang out with his own people. Something I need to point out is that by the time you get t camp you are ready to go home and those that go directly to cam can be considered 'short timers" that is the norm but some at camp still may have up to 9 years still to serve. But my point is that you are trying to get and keep a schedule. You are trying to get a routine. It makes your day much more pleasant and tolerable.

All this guy was trying to do was live his life, h came in alone and that's how he was going to leave, alone. He was trying to get his routine down which makes your sentence go by faster. He had found someone to work out with and he was studying for an exam that he might or might not be able to take because of the nature of his conviction but he was trying to do something, hoe is a great thing to hold onto in prison, so you tend to go out on the limb so to speak to trust or have hope in something. Real estate guy was not bothering anybody he was just "doing you" but that was not enough for some people. I came in from working out, it was after 7; 00pm and it was Thursday, the CO was inside real estate guy's locker, shaking it down.

I never would have thought anything because this guy was a good guy; they fund a phone right on top of his clothes just sitting there not trying to be concealed or anything. Long story, this guy was sent transferred and sent behind the fence, and his stay was graciously extended by eh BOP. The new roommate that was from behind the fence did not like him working out with a black guy, s he tried to pick a fight with him at work, when that did not happen he planted a cell phone in his locker. The guy would not get to see his daughter for an additional 6 months al this because someone did not like something when at the beginning and end of the day, it mattered not.

I will say something about lockers at this point; you would think that in prison you should keep your locker locked, but it's just the opposite, not a lot of stealing from each other goes on, there is some not but not a lot. Many times after 3:00pm you are free to just live and be the four o'clock count is coming and most guys are planning what to have for dinner and some are still working out, some are in the shower. The point, you are free and you leave your locker unlocked and at times you tell your people to go in it and get something, it's just the way it is Also if someone wants something in there, you can show its unlocked and let the CO know that anybody could have had access to it.

I would be remiss if I did not tell you about a real loser and going in a locker. There was a white guy in his late forties that was three years into a ten year bid and he was not happy about it. He had some kids and was in love with his wife, who he constantly said was a crack whore, the thing was that this woman was attractive and I often wondered how in the world this loser got this women. I was coming to believe that maybe he was a dealer. The guy could tell you some funny stories and by appearances was an alright guy, I mean alright for prison, not to be seen with thereafter. I did some typing for him and he paid me always on time without the slightest notion of problem. I regretted it but he had me tying letters to the IRS, the US Attorney really anybody that would respond to him, telling them that his wife was doing things and offering his testimony for a shorter sentence. He was a real piece of work.

Any rate he was the lone white guy with two black guys in the room and he was the type of guy that did not mind getting loud to be herd or to tell a joke or just get attention. He did not like being in the room with the fellows but tolerated it. He was always up to something, he was a smoker and was always going behind the gym to smoke and his finger tips were black because of all the smoking, nonetheless, it was what it was. One day, we had a new boot on campus and he tried to do everything by the book. Walk the floors, shakedown 3-4 lockers per shift, be a presence known. Well one of the black roommates had left his locker unlocked and this other guy had tobacco on him and the guard is walking toward his room so I saw him put the tobacco in the other guy's locker, I saw this.

The guard went into the open locker because during the day all lockers are to be locker, after three you can "do you "it was still before three and he found the tobacco as it was done in a hurry and sitting right on top of his clothes. Well the guard calls over to the guy's job and has him return to the living area and has him in the office. He was a drug dealing smoker but I had never seen him smoke or even want tobacco, he explained himself and because the locker was open the guard let him off the hook. Had the locker not been unlocked surely he would have been in big time trouble and although there is no snitching in prison, I surely would have said something about the matter.

I stopped doing any type of work for the guy after that, I worked in education and could make l the free copies that I wanted and I did not even make this man a copy, I was mad about the situation. Never have I been more aware of my surroundings and the need to really protect myself after this incident. People don't care about me or anything else. It was a shame for me to see this.

You will hear me say the black guy, the white guy the Mexican guys, I am not prejudice at all but in prison the first thing you do in describing someone is say what color or nationality they are. When something goes down between a race of people and another race you better fall in with your car. Your car is your race and nextly the state your are from. If you don't ride with them, you could have issues.

I keep telling stories and I realize I sound a bit stupid or the truth can be questioned because of my behaviors but I am telling you the absolute truth, I acted like a fool. I was naïve to the extreme and in a place like I was I was taken full advantage of, and that is my fault, no one else's. I encountered a group of hit collar guys who had been in prison for some time. It was easy to do so as we worked in the same department, education as a tutor, I was paid $3.00 a month, the older guys were making $60.00 and they were not going to take less for me or anyone else. Hell they made out the payroll sheets the supervisor signed them and turned them in. The guy I am going to tell you about even got the supervisor of education a job, which was why he retired. This guy was an attorney in the world had been chased by the feds three times, he beat the cases the first two times the third time around he got 25 years in prison. Now to be clear these were different charges that he fought each time, so he was no angel in the world and I believe his restitution was over 20 million dollars.

He worked in education and found out that I had a nonprofit and the government had not bothered it. He wanted to come to work for the nonprofit as a consultant and be paid and he told me he could gather millions for us. I was leery because I had not been in trouble before nor did I want any other trouble. I tried to be as nice to the guy as possible but after time and even n the outside it became impossible. You think that people are on the up and up and they are not, you think the title people hold makes them something, it does not. My environment told and taught me this. Because of the fact that I did not cooperate with this guy it lead to my eventual delay in freedom twice I have failed to mention that there are some real cold blooded people in this earth. It makes me want to do better because they are going to burst hell wide open.

On my 18 month sentence I was to do 12 in jail halfway house 3 months and three months for good behavior. I was getting out the end of May/2010. I had written a letter to my prosecutor telling him how unfair it was that I had to pay or be responsible for the restitution of $134,800.00 (joint and several) as I only used roughly $20,000.00. All in the first two weeks of April I get called to the counselor's office and am told to stand in the corner some people wanted to see me. I looked up and it was the prosecutor and two FBI agents, what a way to make your day. My first question was, am I in trouble? Hell, I was told to plead guilty and I would get 6 months home detention that was a lie so believing the system is not something I do easily.

They referenced my letter and told me it did not matter one bit if I testified against the defendant because he did not matter and that it did not matter to the prosecutor because he had been on the job for 16 years and was going to retire soon, but wanted me to testify. He told me that he could not offer me anything in the way of my sentence because it would look like he bought my testimony, but that we could speak after my release about the probation, in my letter I told him that I felt two years was appropriate and he nodded his head and said he felt the same when we met, it was not to be. So I cruised the rest of my sentence away feeling pretty good about my release, my family, my future. Bull Shit.

I got to the halfway house which was/is run by a bunch of ineffective cop/law enforcement wannabe's. I had to sleep on a steel frame bed with a one inch mattress with 6 other people in the room and the TV stayed n all night long it was freezing cod in the room.

Stayed on all night and the stories you would hear, this place was not conducive to resting, but they don't make it for rest, it's an extension of your punishment.

I got a job as a cars salesman the first three weeks I was there, so I was able to get out and get some fresh air most every day. The co defendant's case was coming up and I did not want revenge, I wanted to get past the case and try to shorten my probation. I have to tell you the co defendant gave them every kind of hell you could imagine. He had told me a couple of years earlier that if the feds came out sends them to him; he knew how to deal with them. That always reminded of the Chris Tucker character in the Friday's, see he had mind control over Debo, well Paul was giving them everything they could handle and more then they wanted to.

I never told the FBI where I worked but low and behold one day they showed up and wanted to talk with me about the coming case. I minded it a lot because it made things bad for me at the job, not that I had planned on keeping the job but I needed the income and to get out of the halfway house. They showed up about three or four more times before the trial and I was told by the dealership that I was not that important and could be let go if they continued coming up there, besides that it made me look bad in front of my fellow employees, which I come to understand the bulk had been through the same halfway house. One night a Friday I got a ride from Tim, he took me to the gas station and used the company card to fill out his car, he took me to Kohl's and I kept telling him I had to be in by 9:30pm or else I would get written up, he replied, calm down Rev., tell Rodney I said hello. I was literally blown away. As a matter of fact, my case manager at the halfway house was sleeping with a guy that washed cars at the dealership; I put it together quickly why her car (a hummer) was always clean.

A week before the trial, it was a Saturday, I get back from a test drive and sitting in the customer area was an agent, I was pissed, but what could I say or do? She needed some type of communication from the co defendant and me and ask did I have it, I told her yes, it was on my computer and she told me to search the computer and find it. I called my mother and she brought my computer to the dealership, as you could not have such a device at the halfway house. The morning of the trial I was called down stairs and picked up my briefcase containing my computer and went with the agent. He asked me did I have my license and I told him it was upstairs, he instructed me to go get it, so I got out took the briefcase with me and went upstairs to retrieve my license, not a big deal.

When we got to the courthouse the security told me I could not have the computer in the courtroom, I was needed in court and the FBI agent took the computer back to the halfway house. Listen to me clearly; the FBI agent took the computer back to the halfway house. After court, I was taken back to the halfway house, thinking all was well, I had just done a solid for the FBI and prosecutor, and nothing was further from the truth. Upon entering the halfway house I was told to follow the security guard, the staff gave me a piss test, checked me out with a wand and told me to go to the director's office.

I got there and he shoved a paper in front of me, he was writing me up, giving e a shot from having an unauthorized device without permission at the halfway house. I to this day, cannot imagine such crap. Here the same government that he worked for had asked me to bring it, the agent called and talked to him, I called the prosecutor who I found out had worked with him and he still would not relent, he kept the laptop and still wrote me up. With each write up, your points go up and at a certain scale you are not able to be in the halfway house. Do you see where I am going with this?

I was working, the halfway house sent me home and I did not have transportation to get from my home to the job, it was a 45 mile jaunt each way. We got a vehicle and I was making it for about three weeks. But with all things, nothing good lasts forever, the halfway house case manager would show up unnoticed at your work and require a drug test and just make sure you were there. He did it twice and always wanted me to blow into the device on the showroom floor, I would not do this and this maddens the fellow.

One day, I got fed up with the dealership and went home, my fault, because you have to call into the halfway house when you leave home to go to work and when you get to work and when you leave work and when you get home, you have time specific's about this. Well I walked off made with the world, it just so happened that the halfway house guy showed up and I was not there nor had I called.

I was not up to anything, however, I stopped at McDonalds and got a burger and called the job from the pay phone and the sales manager told me he covered for me and to come back in the morning, thankfully. I called the halfway house and told them I was on my way home, I still got written up, I deserved this one, because I did not follow the rules, I broke protocol. I had gotten a bad hernia while inside and went to the doctor who took me off work as I could not stand for long periods, or sit down or lift more than five pounds over my head. The case manager told me to give him a notice of such and I would be excused from going to work and would just ride the last 5 weeks of the halfway house time at home. I gave the notice.

I got permission to go to the grocery store and run two errands one Friday morning, and I called the halfway house to report that I was leaving, they excused to me leave. When I called back to say that I was on my way home, they told me I had been violated and was to report to the halfway house by 7 pm or the marshals would be looking for me. Can you even fathom that??? I went in and they checked my back in like all was fine, they told me I would spend the last month of my time there at the house. They even let me go home the following weekend on a pass, ok, three weeks to go and this stuff is all over. I could not work, so I am laying in the steel framed bunk watching TV and the punk d. Mann comes into the room and tells me I wanted downstairs, I get there and two U. S. marshals are there with cuffs and chains for me. I would spend the last three weeks in the county.

Did I deserve this to happen, NO, did I put myself into position to be disrespected and told when to go to sleep, when to wake up, what to wear, Yes, I did? It's strange because for all I have been through, it's like a rebirth. See the one thing I take from this entire situation is that I must be accountable. The fact of the matter, I can't blame the co defendant, I did not know what he was doing but I certainly knew he had the capacity to pull crap, I knew what he had done to me, but I made excuses for his bad behavior and a part of me turned my back to the wrong doing, figuring I was not doing it, it would not matter, I could not have been further from the truth, this situation has also taught me to see things for how they are, and to stop lying to myself and others because I refused to see the truth.

I was never more hurt then when my son PJ told me that I was not coming home the Sunday night that they dropped m off at the "hospital" and all he could was to cry, hell I did not even know what was going to happen. The case manager pulled a slick move. I was outside and he came to me and told me he had some past trips he needed me to sign and just put the signature part in front of and acted in a hurried fashion, I signed without looking or reading. Turns out it was a series of "shots" which amounted to my not being able to stay at the halfway house. Also, something that got me was that this guy that was an attorney in northern Arkansas knew exactly what was going. See he got to the half way house three weeks after I did and he had his infrastructure in place. He had been coached very well, but he was a criminal attorney, so he knew the system.

The manner in which staff treated him and treated me and others was night and day. He did not have to call when he left the "company" that he worked for and to make matters worse, his business phone was his own cell phone, strange. His goings and comings were never questioned. I was baffled to learn that after 20 years in prison how he was able to take DAP class, it would appear to me that after that long in prison you would be cured of drug usage, even though you can get drugs in prison. The day after I got a call to my mother, I got a letter from him telling me that I would be out in three weeks and they were not going to charge me with a new case. My mother got a call telling her the same and that he wanted to come to get the accounts and take care of the business.

I believe in my heart and should my lack of cooperation with him, lead to my being brought back and put in county. The "shots" were a small matter and it would not have stood had I contested them, higher more clandestine powers were at work in this matter. When AI got out of the county, I got a call from him apologizing to me telling me that he should have prepared me better for the halfway house and re entry into the world. He said it sarcastically, which really let me know it was him that had something to do with the incarceration.

I had actually never been cuffed and had not seen the inside of the Sheriff's office before. At the county level the feds lease space in the jail for short timed prisoners. The closest I had ever come to being arrested was when I was arraigned and I had to go to the marshal's office to be finger printed, I never sat in the cage and never had cuffs on me. If I tell you nothing else believe this, when I was picked up they put chains around my waist and two pairs of cuffs on me, my charge was 1 count of filing a false financial document, talk about over kill.

My first night at the county was the worst, actually the first three were the worst, the bed was harder, the place colder, it was terrible. I was alone in the cell, and I had no idea what to do and was not able to use the phone, I was worried about my family. The next morning, I talked to a guy that told me he was going to get on a work crew and get his time cut. I waited until the second day of being in the county and spoke to the counselor that came by and told her, she looked at me and told me I was federal and would not be working, she looked at me and said you are federal and made notes. I was moved that night at midnight to the wing that the feds lease that was full of fed prisoners waiting to go home or being sent to the prison to start their time.

I was able to get a guy to call my mother and let her know what was going on and for the call he charged me tobacco at commissary day the following next. Little rat bastard never called he was lying to me all along and I found this out when a guy I knew from prison let me use a phone card to call home and speak to my family.

The first week was miserable for me and my mother could not visit me for another week, but she had money put on my book. County was a learning experience, my cell mate sold his pain killers to a guy across from me for his cake, I learned how to get a message to someone with thread, I learned how to go to the bathroom with a cellmate, and it's called put some water on it. I thank God for my mother, when she came to visit me, she could to talking to the guard that was in charge of the unit, and turns out her uncle were my dad's best friend. Instead of eating at three thirty every morning, back to bed, lunch at 9:30 am and 45 minutes out of the cell, back in until 2:30pm for 45 minutes and dinner at 3:30pm and lock down till 5; 30PM let you out the cell for two hours and then off to bed.

Well I got favor after my mother's first visit. I stayed out of my cell most every night and most days until count time and I passed out the meals and poured the drink, never knew exactly what it was but it was like water for a burning man. My point, after the first week, those last two was a breeze.

I had so much anticipation for my getting out, man I was past excited and I wanted to see my family and get back to life, another bad misconception or pipe dream if you will. The guard I did not care much for rang the cell around 9:00am and told me to get my stuff together and buzzed me out 10 minutes later. I walked through a maze of floors and finally had to change in the hallway to the clothes I had on when I got to county. I was released 15 minutes later and ran outside, my mother was just pulling out and I hugged her in the middle of the street, God Bless I was happy to see her!!!

PART IV
SUPERVISED RELEASE

In the excitement of being free I made a crucial mistake, I had 72 hours to report to probation and should have just gone home and showered and see my son, I went directly to probation. Now this piece of crap was my presentence officer and we had gotten along, so I figured it was not a big deal plus I thought he would be happy as I was for me to be free. They buzzed me in the office and he made me wait 20 minutes before he came out and told me I came in the middle of his meeting and for me to come back in two days. I told him I was happy to see him to, being sarcastic, he told me I was on his shit list and for the next four and a half years of my five year sentence he actually treated as if I was.

Supervised released means you are free to live in society but must live with restriction. I was not into drugs so testing was disbanded, but I had a probation guy from hell. Can a bastard come from hell? Does not matter, we made it, to God be the Glory. I went back to see him at the appointed time and he still kept me waiting for about 30 minutes and when he comes out to get me he has a chicken crap of a smile on his face, so many times I wanted to knock the life out of this man (?) but that would have gotten me more time and it was really what he wanted, my own attorney even told me that probation guy was trying to goat me into hitting him.

So I sit down, still happy to be there and really wanting to distance myself from the past and he starts in on me, telling me what an asshole I am for having done time, how I failed the system by being sent to county and how he did not think I would make it on supervised release, see it was for people who could work within the system and clearly that was not me. My release conditions were a bit of a problem, while some might see them as easy, they were not.

I live in a resort town, gaming, fishing and boating are the main attractions oh and the restaurant industry add to the fact that this is an old boys' network and that says it all. I had a ministry and was able to do well in that circle but I was told I could not work in the industry. My conditions did not allow for me to be self employed and working for a church would not have allowed me to be self employed but he did not want a fallen minister anywhere near the church and told me so. It's a strange thing meant to confuse and disillusion people, see the ministry paid me good money and if you want the restitution paid allow me to do what I was trained to do, don't lock me out of a future.

You say your main concern is that the debt gets paid and you are monitoring every single step I make so why not let me work in my ministry, as it is you are getting my monthly bank statements, my credit report, my tax statements, you know everything I do when I do it, so why not let me work and pay.

This is what happens to ex felons, confused and turned down by the system and unable to get a job because of their record, they go back to doing what it is that got them in trouble in the first place. The system is rigged and it is designed to keep ex felons in the system. See the system has to retain a certain amount of people in it to make it work and that is why we hear about prison reform but it does not happen. People are too concerned about the potential loss of money. People the real crooks are getting rich off the backs of felons and in a hurry to make those guilty when things are not that way.

Why is it that America houses the most prisoners and make corrections a business traded on the stock market, why is it that as prisoners w have to sign time sheets stating we worked a forty hour week and haven't worked 20 hours in a month. You can lie for the system but not to the system and if you do its hell to pay.

I started supervised release September 20, 2010 and was due to be on it for 5 years. I went into it thinking that the prosecutor was going to do something for me as I had testified, even though nothing was promised, it was alluded to so that I believed it was going to happen. I should have known that a man that could sit across from me and tell me that a conviction to him did not matter one way or the other he had a job he was going to retire from. What a statement that is about the government is they so happy to have a job that they get paid for doing wrong that they forget the difference between right and wrong. How in the world in any system will they let you just hang around whether you win or lose cases and pay you a six figure salary? Nobody likes you that much, he flat out lied to me.

The government knew they were going to prosecute Paul but they got me first, figuring that I would cave and do what they wanted. Guess what, I did and they treated me like a piece f crap, there is nothing fair abut criminal justice, not a damn thing, unless you are rich and white. See they could have secured my testimony and held up my sentencing until after the trial of Paul and given me what they said they were going to give me, but they lied and they continue to lie. Instead they made my life a living hell and that of my family for a measly $134,700.00 joint and several.

I know plenty of other guys owing up to 28 million they treat with favor but as the prosecutor said me and Paul did what the white boys did and the FBI did not like that, hell he was the one that brought the charges.

To his credit, at the sentencing, the judge did ask him if he wanted to say anything and he said NO, said if the court wanted him to answer anything he would. When I was sentenced, he asked the judge to allow my mother to speak as my own attorney grabbed her and ask her what she was going to say, what a freaking joke.

My first three months were a bit of an adjustment period and I would go and talk to him once a month, within the first five days of the month. I always made it a point to go the first day as early as possible. He had told me that the ones that have messed up usually come later in the first week as they wanted to spend extra time with their families before being violated for messing up, so I was sure to go the first day possible. I was intent on not messing up, I wanted to do things right.

After the first of the year I sensed a change coming and got an attorney to show everything I did and gave him copies of my paperwork. Actually, I had heard so much about this guy when I was in prison, how great he had been for some guys that I wanted to hire him and yes, I thought he would get me off early and work with the prosecutor to do so. Every month that I would go to probation, I would get permission to make the 52 mile excursion to Little Rock to see the attorney.

The funny thing is, I was in Texarkana with a white guy that was a total slob, had a previous conviction and a dui, he had been a business man and stole from his employer, filed false taxes and was just a total piece of crap not only that, he had the same guy I hired when I got out of prison, as his restitution was 6 times what I owed. Do you think for a minute that they gave him a problem when he got out of jail not a one? They held up his sentencing until they secured his testimony against the guy he ripped off and gave him 10 months in prison of which he did 8. This is a guy with a previous record, a dui, and stole over time over $750,000.00 compared to me, first time offense, no record, no tickets and $134,80000 joint and several, I got double what this guy got and that is only one case I have plenty to reference, the government is not crap but lower. Lady Justice holds whites on the right and all others to the left of the scale and the left is always longer in time served.

Now keep in mind that I had a hernia and employment was not on my top to do list. I had a sick mother, a young son and a wife and I was dealing with the fallout of having been in prison and trying to reestablish myself, so a lot of adjusting was going on. I left my family in shambles. Something the prison system says that they want to do is keep families together during this period and how it effects the children etc. but that is not true, they want to exact every and any once of punishment that is possible and road block anything positive that one might try.

I will tell you that he backed off to let me get myself together or at least try to. It had been a year and I still had not had the surgery that I needed, yet he saw me around the town doing a vegetable garden for an elementary school, coaching basketball through the church, doing a radio show in the city, taking people to and from the courts, my point I as being too visible without any monies being paid into the court system. I thought I was being a good guy and doing good works when all I was really doing was purging myself of the wrong that I had committed and masking it with doing good works, this behavior was not going to be tolerated by probation, I was a common criminal and no amount of deeds goods or bad was going to make me whole. I was going to pay for the wrong I had one and that was through paying my restitution nothing else mattered.

Although I was not working and not getting into any trouble I still managed to send in payments to the courts, it was not much but it was a start. I found a job with a national hardware company that allowed me to work and it paid pretty well. It was not full time work but it had the potential to grow into full time work. I was pretty good at it and they accepted my background, being that I was/am a criminal. After six months they gave me stores in other counties and I was traveling within the state and he had no problem with this as I was not to leave the district without permission but if it was for work he allowed it. For two years I worked like this did community gardens and my radio show, I was a camp counselor for the church and coached basketball; I was easing back into a reasonable life.

Now it was not easy and his visits randomly and periodically did not bother me, I had nothing to hide but I felt a sense growing in the relationship that was not going to be good. The following moth I went it and he told me my file had been picked for review from the Washington office so things were going to change. It's not like we had been friends but he started to exert his title over me and became just overbearing and offensive.

My uncle was being inducted into the Hall of Fame and had invited me and my family, the event was at the Governor's mansion in little rock, being that it was out of my district I asked to go and he grilled me for about 5 minutes as to why I needed to go and how full of shit I was for going to a black tie event when I owed so much money and had not paid any into the debt, how he knew my case was a bad one for him to take just everything he could say to me, he did. Finally he allowed me to go. I was wondering why I was paying the attorney in little Rock $275.00 an hour and he billed me for about 3-4 hour monthly. Now that was another cause of problem between me and probation, he did not like the fact that I or my mother paid the attorney that kind of money, as we were a poor black family He always told me that I should not pay the attorney and just pay him, I should have listened.

The other day I was watching a show on TV, it was one in the line of Judge Judy and Judge Joe Brown, now these shows are indicative of our society or at least they are supposed to be. The plaintiff was a younger male but he had an attitude and was arrogant and the new word in the world, a bully. At any rate, he presented a case that was compelling and he had the victory he was on the right side of the law, his fatal flaw, he was arrogant and it was pointed at the judges and he had a very little regard for the defendant.

He was blatant in his actions and his attitude was on showcase. The defendant who was clearly in the wrong said very little as she knew she was in the wrong, however, she also knew her opponent, she knew that he would implode and let his true self take over the matter and in essence blow the case for himself. She did the best thing for herself, she let him put on his show and not respond to any insults hurled her way by the plaintiff.

After the judge panel started their deliberation in chambers when they had thoroughly questioned both sides and had gotten a clear view of the matter that was before them, they admitted that the plaintiff was in the right and had in fact been wronged by the defendant, however, they did not like the plaintiff and his attitude and they said they could see where he may have even bullied the defendant. The defendant was a young pretty blond and the plaintiff about the same age however, he had means and he showed it. The judges discussed the amount that they were going to give the plaintiff and admitted that they really did not want to do so. They clearly admitted that the plaintiff had been wronged but they could not get past his attitude.

When the judges came out of chambers to give their ruling, one of the judges started to fast talk the plaintiff and really put him on the defensive. Having no shelter or corner in which to retreat, he spoke back in a fashion not was not deemed acceptable by the panel who had admonished him that his utterance of another word would result in his expulsion from the court and in essence he would lose his case. They set this young man up for failure by letting their personal feelings take over and not sticking to the rule of law set forth by lady justice. The young man was banished from the courtroom and the panel smiled in glee as they united and told the defendant that she had won her case.

Having seen this I could and cannot help but draw such a close comparison t my matter. I come to realize that it is not a matter of right or wrong, it's a matter if the system the powers that be like you. Now, I never resented myself to the court as arrogant or a bully or anything other than a humble man that was a minister. Maybe my vocabulary, the manner of my dress and how I presented myself set the judge and those in law enforcement back on their heels and they took me for a threat. Why even the prosecutor told me several times before I testified that I needed to dumb it down because there were going to be 12 sets of eyes upon me and anyone listening to me more than a couple of minutes would know that I was too smart to be in the trouble that I had been in. I have come to realize that the way in which I carry myself makes over people self conscious.

They who had power or control over me in the system knew that in the real world they could not light a match to me had me in their cross hairs and I was going to accept the wrath of their treatment because I made them uncomfortable. Simply put I drew out their insecurities and this could not be. I was going to have to pay for my bringing to surface their bad feelings, of inadequacy and neglect of themselves, heck I even looked good in my greens.

Having had this insight just come to light is a powerful tool for someone, hopefully before they might have any involvement with the legal system, I would say justice system, but there is no such thing, the system is run by a bunch of Hippocrates that are paranoid and confused. If I had gone in to court with my head down and pleaded with the court and told them how bad I had it growing up, my daddy was a womanizing, drunk, my mother ran the streets I was abused by my family and sang a tale of woe, I am sure that my case would have gone differently.

As a matter of fact the woman that wrote my presentence report for the court even ask me to tell her that my father was a substance abuser or that my older brothers and sisters had beat me up or abused me, she ask me to tell her that I drank and abused substances, I could not tell her any of these things as they were not true. She told me that if I could just tell her these things it would make my time in the system much shorter and the judge might even take it into consideration when I was to be sentenced. She told me these things and I had no understanding of what was going on as my attorney did not tell me what was about to happen, as a matter of fact he told after I plead guilty to the one count of falling a false financial document that we had to go and talk to this woman that was going to write u the report on me for the court. I promise you that he told me not to say very much and he would do most of the talking.

That reminded me of the time we met with the prosecutor of the case and he cursed me out for mentioning the watch the prosecutor had and he mentioned my pen. I was sure not t says much. He guided the interview and that is the reason the report contained serious flaws in it. Flaws that he promised me that he was going to correct, flaws that he told the court were misunderstandings when I stood before the court to be sentenced and the judge would not allow them to be corrected which I am told by 6 attorneys that had the errors been corrected on paper I would not have gone to jail. Well he did and the fact of the matter is that I would not have said those things about myself or my family in the first place.

But if I had done what the system encourages us to do my sentence would have been much shorter. It all goes back you don't lie to the court or the system for you will catch an obstruction of justice charge or even perjury but guess what the government can lie with purpose to you all the live long day. I think it was Joe Kennedy that said you send a crook to get a crook. However, we live in the greatest country in the world our government should be better than they are. Much better. I will mention that I was watching the Family Feud the other day, and the survey question was which profession was going to be best represented in hell, the answer, "lawyers". This is one survey question and answer that I actually believe to be true and I agree with it.

It is often said in prison that I love my country but the government aint shit. I have heard that said time after time after time. Something that you are told at orientation is that you cannot win so just shut up and take whatever it is coming your way from the administration. That means that whenever personnel is pissed that they to work on a holiday or whenever they have a family issue they can take it out on an inmate. I remember one Thanksgiving a counselor came to work and he was visibly upset about having to be there. It was foggy and instead of delaying the visits he cancelled the entire visit for the day and that meant that people that had come from many miles away had to go back home without seeking the loved one. That meant that the inmate also went without the visit.

The inmate said something to the counselor and the counselor tried to put him in the hole I can say that the review does work at times, not all the time, but at times. A guard or personnel is not to curse you and if you use the language back it's not ok but not whole worthy treatment. In this particular case the counselor had in fact cursed the inmate and the inmate cursed him back he could not be taken to the hole. I have seen some really unfair treatment and throwing people in the hole and when you get there you are sunk because most f the time they leave you there for the longest period possible. But if they like you, well it's a different story.

There was a guy that snitched on others. I mean this guy told all about the people who were bringing a synthetic drug K2 into the prison. It could not be tested for so a lot of guys were using it. You could tell who were using because they went to work sick and throwing up. At any rate this guy went to the hole with about 12 other people. Now 10 of the inmates were sent to new prisons and were given new charges, they guy and another was the only two to come back. You know they told something. At any rate this guy got his date and it was about 60 days away and he gets a visit from his girlfriend and her just so happens to bring him McDonald's burger. She goes to the microwave and heats it up and takes it to the bathroom, which this joker decides to go in and eat it, well, he was not popular with the guard on duty and he gets busted The visit is cancelled and he is taken to the hole. Now he should have gotten a new charge for bringing contraband into the prison and lesser charge for going to the bathroom without permission, but guess what he only got three days in the hole. It pays to tell on others at times, but I would not recommend it as a full time endeavor.

Some guys, all they do is tell and write cop outs on other guys. I know for one guy a big and fat guy, just a nasty looking guy; he tried to clean up but the underpinning. He was always into everyone else's business. He had to because whenever something went down h knew all about the incident, yet he tried to act cool like he was not involved when in fact he caused most of the administration's actions because he ran his fingers through the paperwork. He was always getting called to the office but no one ever rally said anything to him. It was funny though, one day a guy had been trying to get the chapel for some kind of service, and this fat guy was in charge of the chapel as his job, yet he also had the ear of the chaplain so it was related to me that he told the chaplain not to let the guy have the service. So one day, the guy that wanted to have the service was arguing with the fat guy and they were going back and forth and finally the fat guy just shut up and let the guy have his say, and they quoted the Bible in telling each other off, it was no F.U. or sob you know the regular prison talk it was all Biblical and the guy ended the fight with a quotation from the Bible and told him I leave you with that.

What had happened is the guy went to the chaplain and told him the other guy that wanted a service was not doing it for the service of it, just wanted to get out of work. So the chaplain trying to protect the sanctity of the chapel told NO, the guy then went to the chaplain and spoke to him and told him not to believe the other inmate, the chaplain then told the guy that wanted the service that the fat man was a leak to the administration and causing plenty of trouble around the campus. It all came out during the argument, but like most things, you know who is doing what it's just swept under the carpet until someone wants to have a problem with someone.

Trouble and crap in prison is like a savings account you pull out what you want for a rainy day. Guys are frustrated, have problems at home, hate their cellmates, have no money on their book, their kids are acting up, their parents have died it could be anything because the people are in there together, so on any given day trouble breaks out not fighting just talk and lies, just enough to let other people spoil your day for a day or two or three, but like all things it blows over and someone else is a target.

Speaking of fighting, there was this guy from Nawlin's and they called him N.O. short for New Orleans and he could play some basketball. Tournaments in prison were fun and if N.O. was n your team you could pretty much bet the house. But this guy talked a hell of a lot of crap and he called everybody "my nigga" he called black guys, white guys, Mexican guys, Asian guys, my nigga. He had a cocked eye but he could tell some funny stories and he was always talking or jaw jerking. Well he was on

1st street right across from my room and this guy N.O. kept the lights on in the room all the time, even after it was lights out he kept the lights on and his celli's never said anything. Mainly because it was two white and they were not about to bust a damn thing. He went to court and told on someone so instead of serving another 7 years his sentence got cut down to 12 months.

He came back and they moved him over to the DAP wing, streets 3 and 4. He now had three Mexican celli's and I guess they did not like being called, my nigga's and I heard for about two weeks the cell was having trouble but no one said anything. Along with calling them nigga's he liked to have the light on and DAP wing is a quiet wing, it's a tranquil environment, or so it is said to be. Any rate, N.O. had had words this day with one of the celli's at work and it carried over to DAP class and I guess the guy wasn't going to have any of it that night so N.O. cut the light on and had his head phones on jamming to his music. Next thing you know the celli's had grabbed him up and did some damage, not to his face but his body. Facial cuts and scars would indicate a fight and no one fights in DAP for fear of getting kicked out the program.

He lay up in bed for two days; he got an excuse from the doctor. Without too much fanfare or word, the lights went out and stayed out when they were told to go off, and I do not remember N.O. calling anybody "my nigga" for the duration of my stay at the camp. That was relatively mild and yet the biggest fight, so to speak, at the prison. Another situation that really bothered me was a Greek guy I forget his name but he was a drug addict basket case and a snitch to boot. He called himself dragon but he was a straight up pussy. When people in DAP finish the program they leave the camp pretty much the same week. What they leave behind are lockers or mattresses that other inmates want. This one particular day, Dragon had asked a black guy for his locker and I believe the guy said yes, so dragon takes a cart over to the guys room to get the locker. Now the guy leaving had not told the guy in the room that he told dragon he could get the locker.

The guy was ATL, of course he was from Atlanta, and he was the barber and a damn good one. ATL told dragon he did not have a program giving it to him but for him to wait until the guy leaving came back and gave the OK. This is not unreasonable because you could get into real trouble giving something away without the owner's permission. Hell they get lived about 100 yards from each other, dragon could have come back later, no problem, instead for some stupid reason, he tells ATL "your mother" a senseless comment. ATL being the man that he is hit dragon straight out in the face twice and caused cuts. Dragon being the pussy that he is went straight to the guard's desk and told them he fell. They did not buy it and investigated the matter and ATL got locked up and sent to a medium prison and did not get out on time, how stupid. Dragon went to the hole 3-4 times in a short period of time and only stayed a couple days at a time. This is indicative of how blacks are treated differently from whites and Mexicans and anyone else in the system. It's a crying shame.

Sharing stories, I could go on all day and night, because prison is a fluid situation, however, there are other things that need to be said. I was 2 and 1/2 years into my supervised release and things were changing. He had become more aggressive in his behavior toward me and I on the other hand had become tired of looking at this person. We were making faces at each other, we would be short with each other and it would not have taken much for me to hit him nor him I. My attorney had told me to calm down because he was trying to make me hit him which would have made his job much easier as it was his intention from day one to violate me. I would get to his office the first day of the visit at 7;55am, I would have to wait until the door was unlocked and I would be the first person in the office, he would make me wait until after others came and then he would see them and make me wait, because I did not have a car, he would wait until I missed the bus for that hour and then let me go, most of the time he was trying to argue with me and he would tell me that if I kept pronouncing his name wrong he was going to violate me on the spot, how many ways can you pronounce 'sir incorrectly? The thing is I was working at a nationwide home improvement center and only working about 10 hours a week but I was looking for jobs and could prove it plus I was still very much injured but he did not care.

I was also coaching basketball for the church, I was a camp counselor and VBS teacher, I was active, I figured if I could not work I would at least volunteer my time and try to help others. He was not having any of it, and of course this presented a problem, for me. I remember one time he asks me if I had been to the casino to apply for work, I told him, yes, but you can't have a felony and work in the casino. He retorted to me that he wanted me to shovel the shit from the horses. What I have come to understand is that he wanted me to be disrespected at all costs. He wanted to demoralize me and put me up to see that I was bought down. He often told me that I thought much too much of myself I told him that was not his concern, he would tell me that by having to be under his control I made myself his salve and he was going to show me how much he could and would disrespect me.

A bit of just how bad and contentious our relationship got, because I lived in a different district I would have to have permission to go out of district, this mainly because if you went out of district and got pulled over or in any trouble, they cud put an escape charge on you, and they like to control your comings and goings. I asked for permission to go to Little Rock to look for jobs at various car dealerships, he allowed me to go and requested I bring him back where I went, who I saw and at what time I was there. I took him a copy of the application and a card of who I saw. On the way back home from this job search, I stopped mid way in between Little Rock and Hot Springs, in Benton to get something to eat as I had my mother with me, I could have paid cash and no one would have been the wiser, instead I charged it, thinking this would be extra proof that I did go into town and looked for jobs. He got my monthly bank statements so he knew my whereabouts when I charged something.

As a matter of fact, he even complained to me that I was going out to eat too much and told me to stop it so that I could pay him more money. He used this incident to write to the court that I repeatedly went out of the district without his permission. He court being at its finest hour did not even look over the job applications agreed with probation.

Another incident and this was pathetic, I worked for merchandising company and I worked in Wal mart stores, they liked for me to travel to other store because they said my work was great but I think they were just short on people. At any rate, they had me working in Ft. Smith, AR that weekend and I could have gone the back roads it would have been quicker and shorter, but I did not know the route and instead choose to take the longer way and it was all interstate. Now Ft. Smith is not out of my district, so while I did not need permission to go I went to him and ask and told him where I was staying and each of the three addresses and phone numbers that I was working at. I went through Little Rock and stopped at the Exxon station on Rodney Parham in Little Rock to fill up, it is right off the interstate, and I charged the gas. This idiot again went to the court and told the judge that I was none compliant again without remorse because I continued to leave the district without permission these were and remain out and out lies, but it's ok for the feds to lie on you, but you better not lie to the feds. When the feds want you they will go to any length to bring you down, it can and most likely be built on lies and dishonesty, it does not matter. I often wonder how they look at themselves and if they ever wonder about something happening to one of their own family members...

I have to really calm myself and work not to get ahead of myself. This is a very personal story and for me filled with emotion. I was working part time and going to school, online, he often told me that he did not consider a school that was not brick and mortar to be a school. I was paying the restitution more than the court ordered. I will mention to you that never have I been charged with a new case and I have never been questioned, trouble is not something I get into. He often told me that he never worried about me getting into trouble, he worried that I would get an even break and zoom and roar back to the top, he said I was a convict and my days of good living were over. So the steps that he took did not really surprise me.

It was the morning of my birthday and I had just returned from taking my son to school and was in the process of preparing breakfast for my elderly mother. The time was 8:45am and I was still in the sweats that I had taken my son to school in. I felt somewhere he was watching as if he had become common for me to look up most any place I was and see him. Not that we would talk to each but he let me know he was around. He ask me what I was doing that day to get a job, I told him it was my birthday and I was going to preparing my mother's breakfast and some family friends were coming to take me out and give me some money for my birthday, I mentioned that I was going to pay my restitution with it. I knew something was up because he had his little supervisor with him. He looked through the house and pointed his finger for me to get to my room, which I did. He continues to tell me that I needed a job; I pulled out 14 job applications that I had submitted just that week; he told me it was not good enough. As they were leaving out the door, the little supervisor tells the idiot probation guy that they now had enough to revocate me. I figured all along that they had planned to do something and this was proper for them as it was my birthday. I called my attorney, I will mention this was a high price attorney and he knew the judge that had my case and he always told me I had nothing to worry about well I called him and he told me all was well, I would be off supervision in a year and a half not to worry.

Exactly, one week later as I was preparing to go pick my son up from school, I got an email from my attorney, he simply said, see me about this Friday 10:00am. I opened the document and it was revocation documents that had been filed and signed by the judge. The hearing was set for July 2nd, 2014 making me 14 months short of being free, I knew that I was going back to jail, in the back of my mind, I knew that I was going back to jail. Not that I had done anything wrong or illegal, it's just that when you are on probation the person can do just about whatever they want and if you don't respond as they direct well you got a problem. In my case, it would be a little harder but not difficult. I was not into drugs or theft or anything like that, I was a family man that took care of his mother and minister so the net was not that wide.

I went to Little Rock the first Friday in May and he told me we were going to be fine. He asked me to bring him some papers which I did and he said that we would work it out. But again in the back of my mind, I knew I was going to jail. I don't know if it was a lack of faith in God, my attorneys, or a bigger belief that if the court said something about you, it was true. I think it was a combination of all three and I felt worse because I had given up on God. What ensued over the next two months was letters back and forth and my family complained to the court, the congress, the probation department in Washington, DC..

See I knew that prison was a reality but I also knew that I had done nothing worthy to deserve such a decision. It was in the back of my mind from the first day I was released from the county and went to probation and he told me directly to my face that I was on his shit list. In asking for a new probation officer it was a moot point as the office was small and one guy was just as worse as the other. My next point would have been to go to Ft. Smith which is about 3 hours away, I would have made the monthly trip but they would not allow it. Something that is interesting is the fact that my case started in Little Rock, a different district, I never ask to be transferred to this district and would have preferred to stay in Little Rock, but my plea certainly fell on deaf ears. When you get the law against you, there is no coming back until they reach their desired outcome.

My attorney really got on his horse or so I felt because he took care of everything (to my face) he had letters and phone calls going he was charging me an arm and a leg, which I paid and he was really building my confidence up in him. One day the last week in June, he called me to his office to go over my testimony; again he was reassuring and told me everything was going to be fine. Said if we had to we would take the case to the Supreme Court as there was not any reason to revocate me under any circumstance. As a matter of fact he had even gone to the monthly meeting with me after the notice. He also laid out the possible outcomes and something that stuck in my mind was when he told me that the judge could delay the matter for 6-12 months to give me a chance to work things out. He in essence told me that I was not going to jail and the matter would be put off for 6-12 months and by that time my probation supervision would run out so we were going to be fine.

I was revocated for not working a full time job, for having a credit line that was not authorized and for not being compliant in going out of the district lastly, the probation officer told me to pay restitution from the income tax filed, my accountant came to court and explained that no provision allowed such a demand and my attorney who told me not to pay it for the past two years said the same. I will mention that I had the hernia and the judge told me that he was going to delay the hearing on this matter for January of 2015 to get a status and if I had competed having the surgery, paid the restitution from the income tax that probation wanted, still looked for a job, closed the credit line that I had and not travel outside the district without permission that he would dismiss the case.

During the hearing we made plenty of good points that should have turned this thing around but it never did. See, I was working 30-35 hours a week, the credit line I had was approved by him I just did not get it in writing. I had gotten 4 credit cards while on probation and he told me that if I got a car or truck to get approved for it and bring him the papers and he would let me know if I could purchase it, but if it was a credit card or credit line to get it and give him the paperwork. He told me I was getting near the end of supervision and would have to make some decisions responsively. It would not have been a problem to get the credit line and get his approval for it, he told me to go ahead and if that was the case he should have revocated me earlier in the process. I could not address going out of the district other then with the job applications and hotel stays from the work I was doing, he countered that I did not have anything in writing. Which is interesting because I had a gift card to Ralph Lauren in Branson, MO and he told me to go and would not put it in writing, I never went. See I always thought I was protected because I told my attorney everything, not true. I closed and paid off the credit line within three days of the hearing and paid restitution on the income tax within five days. I was even blessed to get Obama care and had the surgery in Little Rock, on September 17th, 2014. He even called the hospital and hotel where I stayed to verify this was going on.

Something that is interesting is that I was at church camp the week before the hearing and probation knew this. He called the house and demanded my mother have me call him right away for two days. I naturally called my attorney and things got so bad that my attorney got on the phone with the prosecutor and they called probation and agreed that the flow of any documents would come from the attorney, now this was a mission to break me because the attorney charged for this extra work and it was things he had in the file But it got so bad that my attorney told me not to speak to probation unless he was on the line and this o course was going to be extra. Again, I tell you the lawyers and law enforcement gang up and ride you like nobody's business and they share in the profit the attorneys make.

No one can tell me that they are not all in bed together I mean literally and figuratively. After the hearing, I went down stairs for my monthly appointment and had my attorney with me now I had seen plenty of clients go into supervision meeting with the attorney but we got to the door and probation tells us he will not see us together. The attorney goes in first and after about 30 minutes I go in and the attorney sees me at the door and gives me permission to speak to probation. Looking back on it, it was such crap. Something very interesting happened at the meeting between him and I, something I knew would seal my fate. It was never about anything that I had done wrong; I was doing everything right as a matter of fact. He just had what a lot of people have, he was prejudiced and jealous.

The first Monday after the hearing, he started to unfold his plans for my ultimate incarceration. He showed up at my house with a laundry list of places he wanted me to go and a lady that he knew that had great impact on the lives of his felons. Something that always concerned me was that he told the judge on the stand that he told me to go to a place of employment, he told the judge that I said working there would not be a good fit, what a lie, I went there and applied and gave the confirmation to the court, he told the judge that it was no reason I could not work there, when in fact the human resource person told me that they would love to have me but the nature of my conviction precluded me from working there. He lied on the stand, but nothing was said, yet if I had done the same it would be perjury and obstruction of justice.

I went to each and every place that he told me to go to, with no luck; he was sending me on a wild goose chase. I could not even get hired to work on an egg farm in 40 degree temperature and he told me that something was wrong within me. I went to see his employment person and she seemed more concerned with advancing her cause then mine or maybe both at the same time. However, she used him as a front to extract away from me whatever she wanted in his name, over the next eight months, the phrase, Joel would not like that became a tag line in my family's life. She made it seem like I had to check in with her every morning and let her know what I was doing and my whereabouts and in retrospect I guess it was a good thing. He would check in with her and find out what I was doing and she could tell him. I had a good relationship with her, she kept me busy things could have worked out had this not happened.

Something that is a point of interest, she sent me to a place of employment and employed disabled people and she told me to keep my mouth shut to say very little and give them my resume. I did, when I first got there I was asked to wait and the director would come and talk to me. They seemed very impressed for someone of my limited abilities and to function at seemingly a high level, they were happy to have me. When the center director came in to talk to me, she gasped her breathe and told me I was not disabled at all and that is who she hired. The times were so rough for me and a job that I had to go to a dis-abled place and could not even get a job.

Another place she sent me was to the Cracker Barrel restaurant, the job was to clean the restaurant after closing from 10:30pm until 6:00am the next morning. The manager came out to talk to me and I gave her the application and my resume at the same time, only the resume was on top and the application in reverse. I did this because the front page asks about any criminal behavior and past convictions. I wanted to see exactly how far I would get before the water was poured on my interest. The manager was reading through the resume and commented on something's. She mentioned that her father in law was a pastor and we talked about church for a moment or two. She was feeling comfortable and mentioned my education and asks if working nights would affect my schooling. I told her know that besides doing my merchandising in the day I could additionally do my schooling and night work was perfect. I lived less than a mile from the restaurant so things lined up pretty well. She got to the front page and saw the conviction and immediately told me that she had been on vacation for the last three weeks and did not know the status of the opening. She told me that she would call me in a day or two, the phone rang but it was not her.

We were about a month or so into the program of me getting on the track prescribed by the court. I had paid the restitution, closed and paid the credit line which I will mention was a measly $3,000.00, I had my surgery scheduled and I was looking for jobs like no one's business. I worked at a company two different jobs about 15 hours a week, I was in school. The thing is one cannot make someone hire them. Just because you tell me I have to work it does not mean I can get a job to your satisfaction, sadly there was nothing I was ever going to do that would have satisfied these people. What I had done is strung together jobs that made me work 30-35 hours a week, NOT GOOD ENOUGH!!! I got a call from an educational service as a Procter and it paid $18.00 an hour. I gave him the stubs from the three tests that I had administered and he went off on me. Here I am thinking that he would be glad, ok, barely happy or amused that I got an additional position but he goes in on me because I did not tell him prior to working there.

Around this time I caught a break, I had been approved to work as a Hospital/Health Care chaplain, but due to the state of my affairs I did not go through with the position. Funny thing I could have gone through the program when my trouble first started because it took them almost two years to indict me, but I thought I would be acting in bad faith to take the job. But it came around again, and I had to volunteer to the position and in August I would start being paid for it. I went to probation and spoke to the supervisor and he told me that as long as it did not interfere with my job (s) I could go, he then told me to call and leave a message for my officer. I did and the damn guy said he never got the call and that if he had I would not have been allowed to go out of the district like I was going, anther black mark, even when I thought I was doing the right thing.

One might think that I am being overly critical of the person(s) or the system, I am not the things I relate to you are actual and true. It saddens me to think that things are this way but they are. I could complain about all the things that have gone on it my situation but guess what, what has ever happened to me, it has happened to others ten times worse. It is sad things are like they are. Men are losing families because they made a mistake or an overzealous prosecutor wanted to notch years under his or her belt. I don't care how bad a man has been does he deserve to lose his family, get out of prison and go to the halfway house and have to stay there because he has nothing.

It's like the system and care takers of the system have to with purpose keep people down and if they don't like you, they keep the foot on the neck and make every effort to disturb whatever semblance of life one can frame or knit together. You talk about crime and recidivism and guess what the system, causes it. They train you to run game in prison and if you don't make the curve when you get out you end up right back in prison, how convenient, they keep their jobs which they don't do well in the first place and they get to cast dispersions on people just to make they feel worthy. What I am is a bit frustrated. I feel unfairly convicted, lied to by the greatest country in the world, abused by a system that is supposed to be fair and I see justice given to others with money and influence and those that are trying get the boot. It's a saying in prison, if you get in a fight get to your feet and stay there, if not you will wake up with a sore ass. I say this because I know a guy they indicted, convicted and did not freeze and touch his money until after he had paid the attorney in full and situate his family during his absence, he did far more than I ever could think to do he got a shorter sentence and off probation earlier, and he had priors.

During this period of me getting my life together, I took my son to a track meet at his school and wouldn't you know it, probation bastard and little runt of a supervisor came to the house. He asked my sickly mother how my son was doing in basketball and why did she not goes did see him play. Damn fool, the basketball season was over and he should have known it, his son is a couple of years behind my son and they have the same season, hell the entire county has the same season. That weekend I had an assignment to work in Ft. Smith, AR., and it is not out of my district. I stayed at the Hampton Inn right off the freeway and I worked in Alma, and Ft. Smith, two different stores but the same city. Of course the company paid for it and it's the same company that came to my hearing and told the judge what an excellent employee I was. When asked how I got the job, he told them over the internet and that 80% of all jobs now a day are over the internet or word of mouth. The judge said he wanted me pounding the pavement not doing internet searches.

He called the ministry phone number I have and did not leave a message but I got notification of the call. I called my attorney and told him that he called and did they put a warrant out for me because I was working out of town, he said "NO" you are in your district call him and find out what he wants. I called him, he wanted my voice to be taken off the message machine, he wanted the ministry plates I had n the front of the car off and he wanted to know where I was staying. I told him I left that information in his office the day before, he told me he wanted it again, I faxed it from the front desk off the hotel. I think he wanted that to ensure where I was, not that I would have lied, but all weekend I could not get right, I figured or thought a marshal would show up and arrest me. In retrospect he was just hassling me. Another massive waste of government time and manpower.

I got through the weekend and we managed to make it home alright, but I was still a bit off center. I was going to Thursday meeting with the employment lady, we were doing work in the community and I was working as a proctor giving tests for GED and with wal mart add to that going to school. I had completed my masters and was then working n a PhD, I was not breaking any part of any laws and I was paying my restitution. I had my surgery and the doctor did not allow me to work for six weeks but I still managed to work for the first two weeks until my supervisor at wal mart found out and made me call into the human resource office and report the surgery. I did not work for another 4 weeks but still paid my restitution and as much as I could do and still managed to apply for jobs. I can say with all honesty, I was doing all the things I needed to be doing, or so I thought. The employment lady thought so ands she told probation as much, not good enough or as he would tell me, it sucks to be you. At this point I knew I was fighting a losing battle and I started to prepare in my mind for my eventuality, I did not want to but I could not stem the tide or turn the corner. It was nothing I could do.

At this time I had totally lost all faith my little rock attorney and hired an attorney from a national appellant law firm. I felt better about my situation but still I knew anything that I did was futile and that soon, it was just a matter of time that I was going back. The attorney came onto the case and the little rock attorney got beside himself, he shut down communication and just called my matter in, no longer was he interested in me or my family. I can understand him being somewhat upset but if you are putting the client's needs and comforts first, well you make it work after all you are still being paid. To this very day I have had two additional attorneys and the little rock attorney has not signed off the case. Anyway mark was making calls and getting a good feel for my case. The court set aside my matter until January of 2015, going me supposedly a chance to get my life together.

Here it was November, I had just started working at Sears and they promised to keep me after the Holidays'. I was working 30-35 hours a week at Sears working at WaL mart, going to school, giving the tests and going to the Hospital, if anybody was busier than me or showing more of an effort, that person simply could not be found. I was making it work for my family and I was paying even more restitution. One morning I go out to my car and probation pulls up, what really bothered me was that when he saw me he gunned the engine on his Malibu and screeched his tires going to a stop in the parking lot, he jumps out of the car and the dum dum of his supervisor jumps out and runs to the front of the car they are riding in, he comes over to my door and asks where am I going so early. I motioned toward my visor and he nodded at me to go ahead and I handed him my work schedule. He asks me where is my son and I tell him he is sick, he asks me what kind of sick, I tell him sick enough not to go to school. It was not a good moment for me. See he did things to unsettle me and he continued to try and get a rise out of me and he would tell me that he was a Clint Eastwood fan, it did not take much for me to reference the dirty harry character Eastwood had created so no I was not going to make his day.

Throughout this period and my incarceration, my dear son did not know where I had actually been, or so I thought but I continued the story and my family kept up the appearance but you know at times tempers would flare and the occasional slight at my criminal record would come out, he would hear but never say anything. I remember one evening that I was actually at home and the family was there and probation dropped by, my mother is on the phone and walks in the house and hollered law enforcement who is in the house. This again was totally stupid and uncalled for he had never had any type of issue and I am not a violent person, disrespectful at times but he did not have to do this. It was at this time that he told me he needed to interview my wife because he had had reports that I was abusing her and he needed to make sure that was not the case because of so he was going to punish me to the fullest extent of the law. My wife got an attorney to respond to his lies and even the church of which he had been a member wrote a letter to the regard of her not being abused, he went ahead and told the judge that I had been a large impediment in blocking him doing his job.

He also told me that I was beating my mother and taking full advantage of her for her money and he wanted to interview her, hell every time he came to the house he saw her, yet he just wanted to say that I was impeding his case. It was at this time that my mother went to the elected congressman and senator to complain. She wrote letters all around the country trying to bring attention to the behavior of this maniac but no one would listen. Yes they made surface inquiries but nothing would come of it. The things that he would do, were not to the extent that could be traced or tapped it was random his saying that he had reports, well I ask to stand and face my accuser but it was always its confidential information. Just a lie to make his case against me, nothing more. The only thing that really came of it was the fact that when I went for my monthly visits another officer had to be in the room and his comments slowed down but never completely stopped. One thing for sure they sure got quicker. I remember one time the pastor from a large church went to the meeting with me and the supervisor conducted the meeting as the probation guy ducked out. It's strange because my mother had spoken with the head office in Ft. Smith and they knew someone was coming with me yet he was not there. Never tell me they don't pull crap at their leisure. Well the little dumb dump of the supervisor starts talking and says the probation officer had to go to the doctor and he starts talking. He tells me I am too proud to get a regular job that most convicts would be happy to get a job at the spice mixing company he told me to go to. I had in fact gone there and applied, they did not hire me. After the meeting the pastor told me that I needed to shut my mouth, it was the best advice that anyone has ever given me. He told me that they did not like me, did not respect and nothing I could ever say wood change that, so shut my mouth. I took my son to church and told the pastor that I told my son he had given me the best advice ever and my son thanked him. I live by these words and shut my mouth, it's hard because I am a preacher, but it's a must.

A call to the attorney in little rock would result in being put on hold or a return call a couple of days later and then a bill would come charging me for a long phone call that never happened, it was a freaking circus. Seeing the work I was doing one might find a bit of compassion but none was to be had. It seemed like the more good I did the more they would have to dig up to hurt me. Every time I went to the hospital or my mother made a call or wrote a letter it was held against. He even told me that what I was doing was too good for me and he wanted to see me pounding dirt and digging the crap from the local race track. I have to tell you they did a good job at beating me down, hell I was already pretty low to begin with but they worked to kill off any level of self esteem I could muster. I had stopped exercising and my weight totally ballooned, I was looking bad but I kept at it. One day I was in the office of the little rock attorney and he told me that if I had been doing all that I was doing before it had gotten to this level he did not think it would have helped, he told me this guy just did not like me and it told me it was unfortunate.

After the Holidays I was promised by the sears manager that they were going to keep me. Out of my elation I gave him a gift card for his new born; I would have done it anyway. I get a call from the same guy and he tells me how sad he is to tell me that I was out of a job and I did not have to return to sears. He wrote me a letter praising my work. That call came on Saturday evening, on the following Monday I get a call that the hearing had been moved back until May. Strange happenstance, curious circumstance I think not. Probation ask the judge to move the hearing back because I was working at sears when I was out of a job he knew it would be harder to find and establish myself before may, again I was playing in his end of the pool and I was drowning.

Something wonderful happened the same lady that he introduced me to ask me to start working or her. I worked for her about 20 hours a week, I worked at wal mart, I gave the tests, I went to the hospital and I was working on my PhD. Not bad right??? My attorney in Florida told me that the hearing was moved back to may because the probation guy told the judge that he did not have anything on me give him some more time to validate the revocation. I to this day believe that with my entire heart. The attorney in little rock really started to direct my calls to his assistant, a new but capable female attorney She calls me up to tell me that the hearing has been moved because the courtroom had a leak and the judges clerk tells her that this is my time to really start to show the judge what I can do. What in the hell else could I do to show my good intentions. Throughout the entire ordeal I always paid my restitution and never had been in any other kind of trouble again I ask what could I have done? Even working for the employment lady I was making more then when I was at sears as she paid me more, did they respect that, hell no. I can tell you that I tried and believe it or not I was making progress in getting back to myself. The employment lady always exerted me to put my shoulders back and stand tall; she would tell me that I was somebody. She did a lot to help me find myself and we spent a lot of time together I came to depend on her and she was always there for me. She truly knew what I was going through and it was appreciated.

The attorney in Florida filed a motion to have my supervision dismissed, but it was turned down, he filed to have my case heard before May and the court reluctantly had the hearing April 22nd, 2014. Now the little rock attorney started working in just the broadest of strokes, he would contact my witnesses and ask that they were going to be there and send notices out by mail yet I would be billed for a process server, strange. In his conversation with the employment lady, he asked her how I was doing and she replied great, he ask her what was going on and did she have a handle on probation as she had a preexisting relationship with him. She told him that she knew probation and she felt it was time that he retired as he was showing favoritism to certain pale people and great disdain for darker ones. She also went further to tell him that probation had a vendetta against me and she could not understand it.

With everything being out the day before the hearing I am in the attorney's office in little rock and he tells me that he did not believe that I was going to jail, he felt the case would be dismissed. I met the attorney from Florida later that night and we went to dinner, he told me after the hearing I would be in a much better position to live my life, he felt the case would be dismissed. I will mention that I had gotten a job offer from the hospital and it was to start in August I brought the letter to court. I was told that the judge and attorneys were going to meet in the judge's chambers a half an hour before the hearing, this was done to save time and lay out the hearing.

The morning of the hearing, the little rock attorney shows up late for the meeting and the attorney from Florida is in the courtroom waiting on everyone. The little rock attorney shows up and he is stumbling like he was drunk, he did not know a damn thing and all he did was mumble. He did not shake my hand and did not want to look at me. They assembled and went to the judge's chambers. My mother and the employment lady are there and they try to keep me up but I notice the U.S. marshal sitting right by me and he is throwing me some serious shade and looking just pissed at me. About ten minutes later they walk out and the attorney from Florida tells me the judge is going to give me nine months in prison and he tells me that the only thing the little rock attorney wants to do at the hearing is to question the employment lady. You know as good as I do why he only wanted to question her and that was to block out the comment that she made about his being unfair in his treatment of certain people and the fact that she believed he had a vendetta against me.

I am sitting there in shock, I am getting nine months and I am also relived that now I know what is going to happen in my life, unhappy but relived. This total and complete, idiot, prejudiced pile of crap called humanity is out of my life. I am sitting here thinking about all the things that I must get done before I leave; this judge wanted me in jail that day. The attorney did a great job in his cross examination of the probation guy, he had him on the ropes and the court room knew it. It got to the point where the judge told probation that if he said another word that he was going to sentence me to three years in prison instead of the nine months he had planned to. All the while the little rock sat there like he was somewhere else. I could not believe that he was being paid for this he sat there. When I took the stand the first thing said to me came from the judge and he ask me did I realize that I had been revoked from my probation back in July, I replied NO but I was not going to belabor the point the writing was clear. I do not remember if he asked me had it been explained to me or not, I knew I was going to jail, nothing else mattered. Something that always bothered me was that the judge treated the Florida attorney like dog meat, he treated him with little to know respect while he handled the little rock attorney with Kidd gloves and of course he waited until his golden retriever took the stand and they detailed the relationship, the judge sounded and acted like to me a grandfather and they even had a tender moment in going over the relationship. Finally the judge made sure I knew that he was from Louisiana and that he had coonash blood in him, I never ask what he meant or the meaning he seemed to be show boating and I had other things on my mind. What it really came down to was that I had angered his boy and he was there to protect him and set the record straight, nobody bothers his boy. He let me know that the letters written, the complaints made and the objections did not amount to a hill of beans; he was bound and determined to do what he wanted at my cost of freedom.

The judge was so set in his ways to have me pay for whatever I caused and his disdain for me showed. Probation even reported that the amount of restitution I had paid was one number and we proved to the court that the amount reported by probation was incorrect, we did this by simply calling the clerk's office up and requesting the payments made by myself, they differed and the amount probation reported was of course lower then what had actually been paid, the Florida attorney made the motion and included the printout from the clerk's office and the judge denied the motion, here again the probation officer lied on the stand and nothing was done. He works within the court system how easy was it for him to get a copy of the payout, how easy is that, yet he did not. I can safely say that the deck was stacked.

The judge went even further to tell the Florida attorney that maybe after this incarceration I would come out a better man because there was no good in me. The Florida attorney told him that he had come to know me and there was good in me, he told him that I had made tremendous strides for a person in my situation and for that fact any person he went on to tell the judge that I had a family that dearly needed me and ask that he modify the sentence in light of the job offer which would allow me to pay more restitution and since the job was in a different district that the office of probation could monitor me for the remaining 5 months of my court mandated supervised release and that it should not be a problem because no new charges were brought against.

Having said all of that the judge smirked at the Florida attorney and told him he could very well sentence me to 3 years in prison he was giving me a gift at nine months. The judge went even further in telling the court and I that he did not know of any prison that would have me and that Texarkana would not have me back. I can honestly tell you that I have never been written up, disciplined or spent one day or one hour in the hole, nothing, yet he talked to me like this. I did get various write ups when I got to the halfway house in Little Rock, but nothing ever in prison. The write ups in Little Rock were for me backing the car out of the space so that my mother could drive and for having the computer, but again nothing of great substance. But it also shows that he had checked with other prisons and his mind was made up already. He thanked probation for putting up with a problem like me and that was it.

True enough, I had not been a problem for society or anyone else, he always knew where to find m and I did not even get a ticket or anything else yet I am being cast as societal trash and a trouble maker, this makes no sense. Even the sentencing judge told my mother at my sentencing that seeing and hearing her talk about me reminded him of an old Austrian proverb that mothers see their child as faultless when in fact they were troubled. Here again, I did not cause not one problem and yet you talk about me like this. I will tell you this though, I have been told by three current and former federal defenders that when the courts are doing you wrong they put you down and act like you are the worst piece of trash walking.

If I had in fact been so bad why did he not give me the three years that he continued to use over me as a weapon? If I had been so bad why did they wait until 4 years and seven into a five year supervision period to revocate me? If I had been so bad and a risk to society why had I cached a basketball team from the church, been camp counselor and a VBS teacher? Why?? The attorney from little rock had even sent me an email that probation had sent to the prosecutor and we did a community garden for an elementary school and I wore a ministry shirt, he commented that I had a shirt on and he should add into the hearing to revocate me that I was working through the ministry and I was not supposed to be doing so. I was not hiding the fact that we did a community garden for the elementary school to assist with food stability for the kids, he got the picture of me from my own website, and it was not like I was hiding a damn thing. He also had written in a memo to the prosecutor that people like me should not be writing books and advertising them for sale.

The issue was that every damn thing I did I cleared it through the attorney that promised me I was not going back to jail and he told me that he was friends with the judge and the judge would correct things. Make no mistake I was not looking for the hookup or even preferential treatment, I knew I would not get it I just wanted to be treated fairly. Already I was distraught over the fact that I did not go to trial, we had a great case, I was mad that the right for my trial was taken from me, I was mad to being treated in this manner, and I was mad that they used me to testify against the co defendant and alluded to a reduction then laughed at me, but I never let it show and I always treated everyone with respect and this was the case here, even though it was not deserved, respect is earned not given. Well they got it and they still do not deserve it as they are nothing but animals. Wild beasts willing to suck up to the biggest pig in the trough. Yet I am the problem, not in this life or the next.

Just a couple of observations, seeing the little rock attorney in the hall way snuggled up to probation and both of them laughing, not loudly or boastfully but sharing a little joke was enough to make me want to tag both of them. They stood so close together one could not wedge a dollar between them, sharing a moment of two school boys just getting away with something. Looks of pure satisfaction covering the faces of these traders not only to their profession but yet partners in crime. But it brought something to mind. I had reported the previous attorney to the bar for various reasons, I did so because several attorneys in Little Rock told me that he had dropped the ball, but never the less, hearings were set up for the discipline committee and this new attorney was a friend to the one I reported. I was in his office one day and he told me our meeting had to be brief as he had to go to the bar and cast a vote on disciplining an attorney. He looked right at me and I did not get it right away. I came to understand that his vote was the deciding factor in the plea attorney not getting disciplined. I do believe that the mistreatment of my case was in some way payback for my reporting the original attorney. I am not acting in the way of a conspiracy theorist; to me this is real and true.

I will share with you that the night before the hearing I went to dinner with the Florida attorney, we said no to the inclusion of the little Rock attorney. He told me at dinner that he had a fairly large client base and he described a case with a client, he told me that he would do everything within the scope of his power to help his client, but sometimes one could only do so much. He said that some you move on from and others you cry about, but they were few and far between. The day of the hearing, the Florida attorney was poised, professional and prepared. I was impressed by him. After the hearing he made sure that I got down to the car and he made sure my mother was in the car. He told me not to direct some comments that I wanted to make at the little rock attorney and he looked at me and the entire world stopped, he said to me that Jacques I will cry over this injustice and he had tears in his eyes. For a strange reason I felt comfort, someone knew the pain I had been going through. Someone knew and it did not make it right but it better, if only for a moment, thank you, Sir.

The Florida attorney filed and asks that I be given an extra 30 days to report to prison which the judge allowed. He had a thought, because they said my revocation was primarily about my not having paid the restitution, he approached the court to see if the money could be paid if they would allow me to remain free and accept the position offered. We secured the funds in case of the courts acceptance, but to no avail they wanted me in jail. Which really begs the question was this really about the money in the first place. Again, I have to tell you, it was not. This was and remains straight racist activities from the good people of Arkansas, pure and simple. I had a lot of loose ends to tie up and I started to get the things done that I needed to. Originally I was to turn in June 1, 2015 but I was given until July 9, 2015 to turn into El Reno, Ok.. I did most of the things I needed and before I could tell the hospital that I was going away they called me and told me not to come back. They called me on a Thursday, I will not fail to mention that the Little rock attorney came to the hospital on the Monday before the Thursday, he got a tour of what I did and afterwards, he looked me straight in my eyes and told me, Jacques, this job really fits you, but I am sorry that you are not going to be able to keep it. Yes, he called the hospital.

I took my mother to the doctor as she had CHF (congestive heart failure) and she was threatening it again. I believed that we got her medicine together but it was her blood pressure that was a problem. One thing my oldest brother did do was pay for her medicine in my absence. I kept my things together even managed to submit my dissertation for my PhD the Monday before I left to turn in on that Wednesday. Talk about being about your business. If you think watching my mother try to drive the car after not having driven in years the first time I went away, watching my son running down the street after me crying all the way was enough for me to try and escape to another country, to this day, it brings tears to my eyes, to this day the thought of my young, sweet only child running after me brings waves of tears and emotion over me.

The system tells you they want to keep families together, but it's nothing but a bunch of lies and bull if you are a minority it's all about separation. They have this thing called family day and it's where the prison gets dressed up with the cows for milking, painting, the fire truck and they feed you real good. It s a show to get more money from the government, the staff doesn't give q damn about your family visiting they want the money. They feed you the extra food left over from family day until it runs out, they act like they are doing you a favor, and it's a damn joke.

PART V
EL RENO, FCI

I turned into El Reno at 12:45pm as I was to be there by 1:00pm. Without having known it, I caught a break, arriving that late they normally do not process you until the next morning and you end up spending the night in the hole. That did not happen to me, they processed me and I walked to the camp around 3:00pm just in time for 4:00pm count and dinner. I shared a cell with three other black men and this was so very different then before as I had four white men. The bunk was steel and the mattress was two inches of something, but it sure in hell was torn and I was told that I could be written up for the destruction of government property if I did not tell someone. Life was normal for prison this time was worse for me because I had so many good things going in my life professionally, but the good thing was I am no longer under the gun of probation.

What I noticed right off the bat was that the guys were older, the prison sentences longer and the crimes although heavy in favor of drugs, it was a lot more white collar and I had more ministers here. Not that I was looking to make lifelong friends, in prison you don't make lifelong friends, never forget where you are and how you got there and the things that people are after. I have never noticed how closely guys watch what you are doing and get a feel for you and see how they can get up to you for something. Prison is a lie and people lie and the administration lies, yet no one wants to be lied to. My advice is to do your time by yourself, guys are cool to kick it with but never let people too close. You don't want to be drawn into their drama. Please remember if you got no drama fellows will create some for something to do and because of jealousy, prison is a lousy environment.

Your first couple of weeks in prison consists of you waiting for medical clearance. In essence all you are doing is waiting because you cannot get a job until you are medically cleared. Your day consists of call outs and orientation. It's boring and mundane but an evil that has to be gone over. I was in a hurry to get a job as I did not want to be stuck on the farm milking cows or herding them, I have no skills with my hands for electricity, plumbing or construction and kitchen work, well, it is what it is. After three weeks in prison I got the easy job of cleaning the staff bathroom. Never get it twisted because they are staff means nothing, they are dirty, messy and sloppy and don't give a damn how you perceive them, they are better then you and they show it. I remember, the warden and his staff of administrators came down to give orientation and the captain of the Gestapo wanted to make his impression and he gives the tough talk, all you can do is listen. The one thing you really come away knowing is that no matter how wrong they are or how right you are, you can't win, they have the final say so and if they say you are wrong, shut up. Sad but true.

The rush to get your job brings normalcy to your life, nothing else really matters. Once you get a schedule, your time starts to go faster. I use to work out with a guy that had done 13 years and he wanted to work out with me. He always told me, you call it and I will haul it. We got into it one day because I wanted to work out later, hell I thought we were going to fight right there, he got in my face told me off he told me I was disrupting his schedule and he was not going to have any of it. This is how closely people tend to regard their schedule and any interruption brings about something equal to an earthquake. The typical day was breakfast at 5:20am, get your bunk or yourself together, either go to work, or watch TV until you go to work, if you have a call out go to it. Lunch is at 10:00am for the workers and 11:00am for other workers.

Get your laundry put it up; they have a way for you to fold your clothes that it perfectly fits into your locker. Mess around until you go back to work make phone call or check the internet. Talk with your guys or whatever. You get off between 2:00-2:30pm and you can work out before 4:00pm count and dinner or shower and get your laundry together. After dinner you were free to do what you wanted so it's either, TV, walking, working out or nothing, lots of guys play pool and chess. The showers fill up around 7:00pm and the phone lines are busy until 9:00pm which is when you prepare for count. The best days in prison are when it's foggy or something happens in the prison behind the fence because everybody has to go back to their bunks and stay there. It's always down time and if you get along with your celli's you can talk a lot of crap, it's fun.

Here is an example of my day, minute for minute: I would wake up at 4:45 am get myself together, take my laundry and get in line for breakfast, go back to my room and take whatever fruit they served at breakfast and put it under my pillow and put ice on the milk that I had in my pocket as I left the dining hall. I would then go clean the staff bathroom and then go and pray. It was 6; 15am by now and I would get in line to check my internet messages and call home to speak with my family before they started their day. It's 6; 45am now so I take my clothes off and go back to bed until 9:00am that's when I walk or workout most days I stayed in bed until 10:45am and ate lunch then got back on the internet or called my mother to speak with her. Calling home was important to me and problematic at the same time because you only get 300 minutes a month n the phone and 400 during the holidays.

After lunch I would go back my room and read and the church to pray. I would get my laundry and put it up and wait until 2:00pm to work out and come in by 3; 45pm for count and dinner. I did not have to go into the dining much for dinner as I had a guy cooking for me so many days I would go back out and walk or do some dips. So by 6:00pm my day is over as I would take a shower and usually eat around that time. I would usually do the dishes and pray for awhile or go back to my bunk and write sermons or read the Bible. I would call home for the night and then check my emails. That is my day until 9:30pm count which is over by 10:00pm the cop clears the count and I would go clean the staff bathroom and be back in my bunk by 10:20pm, which was my day.

A couple of things come to mind. Could they not have found a different solution to unjustly punish me for the nothing I allegedly did instead of costing the tax payers over $35,000.00 for that nine month incarceration? I mean I told you the high lights oh I forgot, my big day of the week was going to commissary every Tuesday, Wednesday or Thursday. I had bills to pay because I paid a guy to clean up the ice room for me and I had a menu for the guy that cooked for me to get and most of the time I would go off the reservation and owe the store man. It was a mistake to owe the store man but for me it was the closest thing I had to life in the normal way. I enjoy shopping and spending so this kept me on center, hell of an expensive way to go about life but when in prison you do what you can to stay the course of life and its free form. Something about me, I never lived not one day in jail, my mind was always free and I never concentrated on prison or who was there, I lived on the outside and kept my mind in the free world. To some this was wrong to others it pissed them off, I did not care, I was going to live how I did in the world and it caused problems but I did not give a damn, I came in alone and I left alone nothing else mattered.

In retrospect the only thing I really missed was not getting a MP3 player. I had a watch a radio and a fan the first two weeks in prison and I was there for 9 months and my roommates told me it was not long enough time to make the investment, that is the only thing I should done that I did not do, because music was my escape. Some many nights I would go to sleep with the ear buds in my ears and wake up around three in the morning and not be able to get back to sleep so I would just lay there. But it was the way of my life and not much to deal with considering where I was. I will tell you also that when I got to camp I was severely overweight and had a blood pressure problem. My norm was 155-165 over 95-100 so it was high and adds to that the miserable conditions in prison, it was hot as hell. I slept on the top bunk and many times did not want to get up. So I slept in the day as my nights were restless.

It took the medical staff about 6 months to get my blood pressure under control and it took 5 different medical prescriptions to get it there. Many days my head was dizzy and I had dry mouth. My blood pressure and soft shoe pass allowed me to have the job I had. I think it took so long to regulate my pressure because the staff doctor was very inept, when I say very inept, I mean it. Now this is a rumor and in prison lies and rumors are the standard, but I heard that the doctor had had his medical license revoked in four states and the joke was that he was the prison's highest paid employee. Now whether it's true or not I am not sure but it kind of fit the situation.

Around the Holidays we had a couple of guys walking around the prison saying pay that, whenever you said something that as off the wall or inept or if you answered a question not directed at you and it was wrong just stuff like that. I thought it funny for a while and of course if you were late in paying up, this was done by pushups, the marshals would come get you and exact payment. Some cases they would hold you down, it was all suppose to be done in good fun but sometimes it got a little out of hand. You must consider the sources of such of the root of entertainment. Generally guys that have been in prison for awhile get a little bit restless and resort to ways to keep themselves up as it gets boring. Guys that have been behind the fence are use to a much more structured way of life so when you get to the camp it's an entirely new day it feels like freedom, so are prepared and some just are not. I know of a couple of gentlemen who could simply not take the camp and wanted to do something to get caught so that they could go back behind the fence. I was never there and had no desire to do so.

At any rate we had this guy name Burrell, and he was a funny sort. Now he had been down 2 previous times and he would have been careered but this was for drugs and the other were for fraud, or at least that is what I am told. He was smaller but had the longest hair and no offense but he was ugly, had the nicest white teeth though. He had been around and generally was a nice guy. I had been moved because someone was jealous and told a lie to the counselors so they busted my room up. Any rate Burrell became my new cellie and he was a very particular guy. We had a white guy move in and Burrell acted up so bad that the guy moved within three weeks, it was not that he acted up but how he acted up, he did not want noise in the mornings, but yet would bother you, he wanted to sleep late on Saturday when everybody is up but wanted it quiet.

The funny thing is that he had been kicked out of Leavenworth camp and wanted to get back there for DAP. We actually prayed about it for sometime but it was no use, no way in the hell was he going back to Leavenworth. He was sent to Wisconsin to complete his term and was unhappy about it. Happy to be moving on but unhappy in moving. He told me about the time that he was in prison near Mexico, and he was watching TV and I guess this guy thought Burrell had told something on him, so he is sitting there watching TV and the guy from what I understand was at least 7' tall, and all of a sudden Burrell tells us the guy says say I won't and then hits him right in the face. Burrell knew that if he got up the guy would have thought that he had gone and said something so he said that he sat there and watched TV with his glasses half way up his face and blood on his lips. Burrell said that later that night he called his brother and they both cried on the phone because he could not and did not do anything. It's a part of prison but the way in which he told the story had me rolling on the floor it was funny. Anyway Burrell was always into something and some day's guys would be chasing him down to the cell, not to really kick his ass but rough him up a bit and the next day he was right back at it. He was a true character and really stands out in my time at Camp El Reno.

In a great sense he was indicative of most of the inmates there. He was older had been in prison previously and was just tired of the grind of prison. It is at this point that guys start to get a bit anxious in their behaviors. I don't know that it is a good thing to continue to mix, long time career criminals in with relative low termed white collar guys. My point is that there needs to be a better mix for the system. Now you can't just make a massive change in the system, or maybe that's what is needed, but it would go a long way making things better. For instance, you get to come to the camp when you get under ten years remaining on your sentence. That in most cases means you have been behind the fence and have acquired certain manners of behavior that a traditional camper would not understand and the result is sure friction. For instance, the TV room has six TV sets and they are programmed for Mexican, Black and White and then there a room for Mexican TV, a Spanish speaking channel because you have guys in prison that cannot speak a word of English, or so that is the tag line.

My point, the guys talk in the TV and it has tendency to be a very caustic situation and loud. Some behaviors which are the norm for some are unheard of for others. At any rate there was a problem in the TV room someone got knocked down over a program and the response from the administration at first was to shut the TV room down, it's a response because some of these guys live off the TV, next they took the chairs out of the TV room and the guys then started to take the mattresses off their beds and lay them down on the floor and the administration did not like that so, while its always an us vs. them mentality at times the situation is resolved with the administration giving in. my point, the administration tries to keep you on your toes, constantly, they want to keep a great amount of pressure on you and the prison, it keeps the environment like a power kg and that is what they want, see if your enemy is poised to strike you know exactly how to deal with him and work to control the situation on every level and turn so when you get to the point of break they are already there and doing something else.

They try to keeps to steps ahead of you and control you even more.

Something that was very different from El Reno and Texarkana was the system of things. Please know that to an inmate, the last place they were was the greatest place in the world and they are always saying when I was at so and so prison we had this and we had that and this was how it was done. As for this place it's a piece of shit, etc...... But the thing is across the board the places are ran the same and the menu's are even the same. I don't know that they are ran the same but I heard from one guy that was sent to another camp, they had a movie theatre aside from the TV room and they allowed you to have popcorn and other treats in the theatre which I find interesting. I know that at Texarkana we had microwave ovens and at El Reno we only had hot water no microwave oven this was an administration thing I don't think it was a system thing. My point, the administration has a lot to do with how the particular prison is run. I believe the administration at El Reno were not as seasoned or prepared for the adequate running of a prison. Here I am comparing the places, but Texarkana was a much cleaner prison and we had microwave evens in which to cook and the Holiday meals were better. Aside from that not more of a difference other then the administration.

El Reno kind of blew my mind, the 10:00pm count at Texarkana was now at 9:30pm and the thing at Texarkana you had to be standing straight up and nothing in your hands no radio in your ears just standing straight up, at El Reno, the count was not that big a deal you could not make noise to disturb the count but you could stand there and read or listen to music some guys even played chess during count. I want to share with you an example of the sheer abnormal and idiot nature of people. About a week before I left the camp they started to sell bags of cereal on the commissary, good enough as throughout the day and especially at night it would be a good thing for prisoners to have as a snack. Well the administration puts out a warning that anyone caught with milk and not having the powered milk that they sold on the commissary would be subject to disciplinary action. Now in the mornings and sometimes at lunch you could go to the dining hall and take a couple of bags of milk with you, El Reno has its own diary so the milk was always provided. Or you could be friends with a diary worker and he would bring milk home at night. The point is you could always get milk but the administration did not want you to have the milk provided they wanted you to buy the powered milk they offered. Who in their right minds would want to have powered milk over real milk, especially in there cereal. Why in the world give it then control the flow of it. I don't even want to hear the argument that it is considered contraband because on holidays and special days at the prison the administration gives you a box of food to eat in your own room and it's not considered contraband its considered a gift by the administration. And don't stop there, they call their days and give you a very unfulfilling box lunch or dinner at 12:00 in the afternoon and it's ok. My point be consistent and not hypocrites.

The thing that never changes about prison is the fact that people read. Their people send in books and usually after you read it you pass it along something else are magazines. Guys are rated by the type of magazines they get in prison and newspapers. It's a regular circuit of circulation. When the original owner finishes the newspaper he will give it to another ho will in turn pass it along, the same to a certain extent goes with magazines, you pass those along but you tell the person to remember where he got it from and not to take pages out of the magazine. Gossip magazines are more available than any other because guys have a sense to need to stay up on what's going on in the world. Guys also make it a point to watch TMZ; they crowd the TV like no one's business. We had this one guy that was there on revocation and had been revocated for 7 times, so he knew how to do his time and get along with people. He could make the funniest comments and one day this guy was really making on over one of the famous K sisters and they were featured in this magazine, the guy is begging for the magazine and finally he gets it, he wanted to take a certain page to the shower, and the guy that had been in and out of prison says very loudly in his radio voice, hey nigga this magazine aint mine you can borrow it but just don't jerk off on the mutha ******! Man the street was rolling with laughter. Just another day in prison.

Funny thing, the female guards always think they are sexy, even though they are not, by long shot. We had this one guard with a feathered hair style ugly face but a nice body and when she did count she would put a little extra twist in her hips, hell, I hope she did not walk like that in public. One night Burrell said he was going to screw with her, he had baby rattlers, he would call them, they were guns and he was posing showing off his baby rattlers and he hit mid pose as she got to our cell, well she stops and gives the most flirtatious smile I have seen in some time and asks if everything is ok within the cell, at Texarkana that crap would be shut down and Burrell would be in the hole, without a doubt. That is a difference in the administration but for the most art the prison is ran the same. I will say that the people in El Reno seem a bit unprepared to run the system to be effective and run like Texarkana, which seemed to run smoother and be professional. These people seemed to want to be your friend if they liked you and your enemy if they did not like you. If someone said something about you they had it in for you whereas in Texarkana everyone was treated the same, like a piece of crap but there was no gray area El Reno it was the time of day or how one guard felt that determined how you were treated. People always say well maybe there wife did not give them any last night, who gives a damn he has a wife to go home to, I got you to look at.

I remember I was taking a class on criminal thinking and the inmate next to me was complaining about having been lied to repeatedly by the administration and then he was complaining about the behavior of a guard and the instructor says to him, you don't know what is going on in his life maybe he is going through a divorce and his wife is taking $50,000.00 off him, you never know. My point, is that my fault or concern? You get paid to do a job, paid very well because in the real world, you could not make it. Do not bring your problems, real or otherwise to work and take them out on people just because you can or want to. Don't take them out on people that you know are not the cause of the problem and then know in the back of your mind that you can get away with it because of the position you hold. Don't be a dick just because you can be. Unfortunately most are and really don't care that they are, it's a pretty sad commentary that you pick on people that can't fight back, and the world talks about bullying, go to prison, it's not the prisoners it's the staff. The problem is that they always think the inmates are up to something, they don't have to be but it's the perception. I mean after all why the inmates here are, they got caught with their hand in the jar of cookies so you are not trusted and treated in a fashion that is disrespectful. I remember one day I had team meeting that's a meeting with your counselor and case manager and sometimes the camp administrator. I was in the criminal thinking class and they had to come get me out of class for the meeting. I apologized for being late, because some people had been sent to the hole or even fired from their jobs for being late. At any rate the female administrator asked me did the class stop me from thinking like a criminal, I told her we all at one point another think like criminals the class is designed to help as see another rational approach to our situation. She goes to tell me it was pointless for me to take the class. The thing is the answer I gave her is directly from the text folder, go to hell lady.

I did have a counselor that I considered new to the job; he was alright and said that we would get along because he was educated as I was. I could go to him and he was fair to me, he was reasonable and patient but he did not want any crap. He told me that he had never caught me in a lie and as long as he did not he would treat me with respect. That was refreshing as a lot of people around the camp were full of crap. However there were guys that were earnest in their attempts to do the right around the camp, those were usually guys who were resigned that they had a long way to go in their sentence so you might as well start now. Resentment is rampant at the camp. Resentment of everybody and everything. It is important to remember that ho you are in the street is exactly who you are in prison. If you ran your mouth in the streets you talked a lot in prison, most of it lies but no less you were talking. If you were on the move in the streets, the same thing in prison you walked up and down the halls running game and making deals.

We had this one guy named Buster, he seemed like a real gentle soul but he was a shark at heart. I understand that the feds took a lot from him and he has various cases which meant that he was going to do some time I think about 7 more years. He had a thriving glass company but he did a lot of real estate on the side, and I think his trouble was that he rode the line to closely and just go over the line in the world. From what I understand his wife left him and it broke his family up. Not sure that he had anything to look forward to but you never know. In prison he was kind of like the man to see about things. He had a way of getting up to you to get in your favor but he turned very quickly to his usual self and that was selfish and all about him. He would take from you and give to others, his inner circle to keep them happy, I don't really blame him, and he was going to be with them a lot longer. He had roommates that were in need and he made deals with others all over the prison to get things done. I mean he had truck drivers bringing in watches; he had others bringing in protein for the body builders he had a lot of things going on. One time his roommate got caught with contraband that Buster no doubt had brought into the prison and the roommate gets shipped, they gave Buster a hard time because they knew he was behind it. Buster was good because at the end of the day they could not prove it but they hassled him everytime they had a chance. If it rained outside it was hassle Buster day, if something went wrong in the kitchen it was hassle Buster, now he did bring these things upon himself but it was over kill. I think what pissed the administration off was that he had a great job and worked very little it was a job of privilege they made him quit the job. This was telling because if you are cleared to work and don't they can put you in the hole or ship you out, Buster rode a fine line. Whets more is that he started to become sloppy in his dealings; he taught he was above the standard and he taught he was above everybody around me. He kept a book with detailed notes, I am glad it never got into the hands of the wrong people.

I got my watch, radio and fan from him. My cellie's were pissed that I got the fan because it was the fan of the roommate that got shipped by having the contraband that Buster had arranged. I did not know the guy and it was a business transaction for me, not a big deal. The watch he had sold me was from the free world and he told me to take it off when I went to see my counselor as I would not have been able to buy it on commissary and I wasn't there long enough. Wearing it would have brought attention to that fact and as you cannot get anything from another inmate prisoner, it would have lead directly back to him, trouble he nor I needed. I felt sorry for the guy because he did not have any money, and whatever money came in he because of restitution had it taken so whatever money he had it was from his hustle Not a good way to live in my opinion but that's me, I certainly had my own great share of issues to deal with. My point, the system does not take you far from who you are. It's kind of sad to see someone have to go and be on the go and not take time to think about what caused them to slide to the situation they are in. I am not excusing or denying my faults or problems, I can say all day and night that the co defendant did everything but in my heart of hearts I knew he was up to something, I simply turned my back. I instead went to an attorney and laid out what was going on and did what he told me, after that he said that nothing coming against me could stand u in court. I took comfort in ducking my head in the sand I knew I was wrong. Sometimes things get so bad that you turn a blind eye to what is going on and as a criminal you always try to out run the situation or think you can turn it around. But, anything you have to outrun or try to get more time to satisfy is nothing but a different version of a ponzi scheme.

People in prison unite under the same or similar circumstances. The people that were down with each other at El Reno were truly unique and had a bond formed that was lent itself a great notion of support. I had problems fitting in and when I extended myself I handled the situation incorrectly, remember I never let my mind or soul exist in prison, I looked to the outside. I was in a different position than most, my time was short and my supervised release was over, many guys upon their exit from prison would just be embarking on supervised release so it was a different situation. I can and will also tell you, I can be difficult to get along with. I like things the way I like them, I will wait to have things my way and I had money to do whatever I wanted and I was not afraid to make it work for me, many guys did not share the luxury I had and while I did not brandish it, neither did I cover it up. Many times I said that I was going to enjoy this experience because it was going to be my last time on this merry go round. Again, I had a permanate place for my foot and that was in my mouth but at some point I just did not give a damn, that is regret, but one I will lose no sleep over. I had my future in hand with two very good job offers under my belt. They seem to have not gone as planned and I will not be working for these companies but it does not matter I have a ton of options. In prison however, I was under the impression that I would be moving directly out of prison, it did not work out that way, it was comfort for me while in there, but now that I am out its better this way.

When I was in Texarkana I never moved from my room no matter how things got in terms roommate differences and there were several, I have always been somewhat defiant regarding things and can be difficult to be around, but at the end of the day, things worked out. I lived in three different rooms at El Reno the first was where I should have left from when I got out, it did not work out. The second was with the character and after he left, things got out of hand. People are manipulators and always angle to have things the way they think they ought to be. They are liars and thieves and think they can get away with anything, but they must remember that is why they are in prison. I have said it all along; you got the sentence you got for a reason. The longer the sentence the more of a problem you have been and that will not change. Based upon the actions of these people they will end up back inside for another version of what they did the first time around. A problem that I have is that I cannot look at a situation and see the ability to manipulate it I come straight down the middle people and the last room I was in before I moved to the final room have a way of making things what they what them to be no matter the cost. In prison people know who you are most to all of the time they let you be who you are because they keep it moving and don't take you into the circle of confidence but the common bond is that you both are in prison, some guys violate that soft bond to get what they want. It's a true sign that you will be back. The last room I was a cool room for I was there for 13 days.

The guys were cool and if I had known the dynamic I would have moved there on the initial move but things happen for a reason. Something I never really got the hang of was that people in prison could talk about you behind your back and I mean really talk harshly about you and say various things that are not flattering and then in the same breath see you and act like you were cool with each other. Like you have been friends for years. That to me is as two faced as it gets and guys do it every day all day. I can honestly tell you that I did not like that, if I had to talk about you, I did not care who I send it to because I did not have a problem with it getting back to the person I said it about. Guys in prison talk a lot and they may need something in the future so they keep things on the cool. Not I if I had to say something it was said and if I talked about you believe me I was not your friend and wanted nothing from you. Period. Does that make me better; no it just makes me who I am and the fact that I was not there very long contributed to my behavior. One guy came to me talking about wanting to change and being a man of integrity and not listening to rap and just being about his, well when other people came around he would curse, to not be a man of his word and listen rap, which it's nothing wrong with that but he was just a LIAR and he thought he was better than people it's a shame how people get mixed up. I can understand how he could be mixed up he was and is a has been with very little to look forward to, I feel sorry for him.

When was leaving that morning the guard walking me out ask me what was the first thing that I was going to do, I looked at him and told him that I was going to put on some proper clothes and go to Cattlemen's for a steak, some eggs and biscuits and coffee. He looked at me and told me that most guys tell him some pussy or something like that; he then told me that mine was the best answer that he had gotten in the 7 years he had been on the job. I went to Cattlemen's and did eat my meal, I will tell you, I have had a steak in almost every state and this one was by far the best I ever had.

At any rate the short time I spent at El Reno had come to an end. It was difficult as there had been so many moving parts and so much confusion going on in my life and the life's of those around me, but none the less it was over and I was so thankful for that Friday morning. I got the best advice from someone that a lot of people were skeptical of the night before I left, he told me that I was not to be ashamed of anything that I had done in life, and for God knew that I would do as it was written in the book of life. How I dealt with it in the future was what had mattered. I knew then that I possibly should have interacted with him a little more or maybe just had it like it was either way, I had been blessed. You never know how people will impact your life but you need to stay open for disclosure.

PART VI
THE FUTURE

My day came that I was leaving El Reno and in my heart I knew and know that I will not be going back. This prison term was harder than the term at Texarkana, mainly because I was older, I knew what I had put my family through and they needed me, I had done a lot of things toward improving the future of my family and I was feeling bad that I had left them. I was being selfish because for all that I had done I still had an issue that needed to be dealt with and I was not yet up to dealing with it. You cannot serve two masters and soon enough I was not going to be. With all that being said my future was still bright and I was going home, God was and is in the plan. The last thought, vision I had of home was that of my son running down the street chasing me, he ran until he could run no more and then he just broke down crying that moved me to pull over in the street and go to him, pick him up and put him in the car and we went back to the house where he refusedt o go into until I was out of site. I still cry at the thought of my behavior doing this to my family.

I released on a Friday morning and got home on Monday morning. My son had been waiting and greatly anticipating my return. He did not go to school that day and it was raining when I pulled up. I got out of the car and the next thing I see was my son charging out toward me, he was bigger then I remember and he was happy, crying and smiling all at the same time. You talk about something moving your heart; in all of my bad behavior here was my son here, just waiting for his dad, who he loves so much. We got inside the house and guess what the Christmas tree was still standing, a real tree not a fake one. It was dead and had seen much better days but it was there and to my delight presents were still under the tree. How many people can actually say that they had

Christmas in April, I am sure that some can but for me it was some kind of special. Another thing, guys getting out have no concept of family dynamic and holidays to exchange presents, as they have been in for a minute, I was gone and returned after nine months so my family dynamic was still pretty much put together. Calling home and emailing as much as I did helped.

I am thankful to have my life back and my family in order. I remember still being concerned for my mother when I was on the inside and about 6 months into my sentence I had a dream that my mother was lying on a stainless steel slab, we know what I am saying here. I called her up and told her that I had a bad dream about her and that I needed her to take care of herself at least until I got home so that we could fight some more. Mom tells everybody that she is living for her grandson, it's not her only grandchild but she acts as if it's her only child. I understand that he, my son, PJ is something that gives her life so she holds on a bit too tight but if that is all I ever have to worry about, I really have NO problems. She did her usual thing and laughed and told me that she was going to hold up until I got home.

Well after I pulled in that Monday, we went out to eat and went grocery shopping and had a great day at home. PJ went to school that Tuesday and sure enough Mom held on as she had promised and we went to the hospital and they kept her. It was her heart and she had fallen back into CHF, she was as swollen as much as any time that I had seen and her blood pressure was sky high. She in fact had not been taking her medication as she was prescribed to do. She had been worried and half out of her mind, but she held on. She was at church and a little girl had run in front of her and cut her off and mom fell flat on her face and was agitated for some time.

I am enclosing a picture of her face but her spirits were broken. She told me that if I had been here she would not have fallen. Not altogether true but I go with it. Her hospital stay was 10 days and she started feeling better after about day 6. They had to get a handle on her blood pressure and her swelling was managed but did not really go down like they would have liked. Day 7, her blood pressure dropped and the water came off quickly. So by day 10 she was on her way home. I believe that to be a Friday afternoon, she was happy but has been a step or to slower. We went to church that Sunday and I called her to tell her we were going out to eat and ask if she wanted anything, to which she said no. That in and of itself should have been concerning, for mom always wants something brought home. We got home a little later than we expected and knocked on the door as the screen was locked. No response, we knocked and then called for about 5 minutes, no response. I could see mom sitting in the chair and it was at this point that I pulled the screen off the hinges and unlocked the door.

Mom had passed out her skin was pasty and she had thrown up on her gown. She had an attack and was not looking well. PJ called the ambulance and they came right away and took her to the emergency. Mom ended up staying in the hospital another 10 days. Her weight is down and the swelling is big as ever making it difficult to wear shoes but she has not recovered as she is much slower and her blood pressure which used to be 117 over 65 is as of the writing of this book is 139 over 79. It's inching up and that's with the newly prescribed medications given. Not sure what to do because three doctors have her coming back in 6 months ....

PJ is a great child and if I sound partial it's because I am. He has all AP classes and is on the honor roll and he plays basketball. Not great but he plays and can shoot his tail off. Great kid and he has fun in just about everything he does. Something that concerns me is that he stays on the darn cell phone all the time. We spent a good part of the summer traveling to his basketball games and he did well, he understands no scholarship for basketball is anywhere near the horizon but he sings and has had three solo's at the concert choir and that for sure is a better option. He seems to be well adjusted and happy and that's really all I can ask for. He loves to go to church and the only problem I have with PJ is waking him up. I tell him all the time that the best part of my day is seeing him in the morning and the worst part is waking him up, it's always a struggle.

Back about 8 years ago, we had a driver for my mother. I was in and out of town on a weekly basis and my family needed to get around so I had a cab driver to pick them up whenever they wanted to go somewhere and we would settle up at the end of every week. He was a nice man and a wise man. He was good to my family and I can only hope that we were as good to him as he was to us. Bill took sick and had to stop driving cab. I will tell you that before he took sick he drove my mother to Nashville, TN twice to the doctor, which is how we found out she had cancer. He never complained and was always there for us. He had take the family to wal mart and stand by the door because PJ liked to run around in the store and Bill always said that he was so good looking somebody might try to keep him, he called PJ Sir PJ because PJ was and remains the focal point of our family. Well when Bill got sick he did not know that we knew here he lived and one Saturday afternoon we went to his house for a surprise visit. Bill always liked frosted flakes with Neapolitan ice cream, at least that's what he told us, well this day we took him 5 box of frosted flakes and five cartons of breyers Napolitano ice cream. We did not tell him that we were coming but we call 5 minutes from getting there, no answer. We drove up to the house and he was out in the yard and I promise you that he did not know who we were. He started for a rock as he moved closer to the car but when he got closer he recognized mom and Sir PJ and he laughed out loud. He invited us in to the dismay of his wife. She told us that we were the first black people ever in the house. She was being insulting but we did not carry it too far, Bill was a gentleman and we were there out of love and respect for him.

I tell you this because he drove me to plead guilty. He knew the stress I was under and told me that a trial would almost kill my mother and depending how long of a sentence I got she might not be around, but he told me if I wanted to fight he supported me all the way. As it turned out the plea was the worst thing I ever did, but it happened. I mention Bill to you because we were out to lunch one day and he told me that he had not slept well the previous night, said that he was not sure why and it was nothing on his mind or his conscience bothering him. I told him he just needed to eat a meal with me and he would sleep well that night or have relations with the wife, either one would do the trick but his wife was the better option. His words have always haunted me; see for years I have not slept well. I mean before all the drama of this case started I did not sleep well. Certainly after the knock on the door from the FBI in 2005, I did not sleep well and I have not since then. I know some guys in prison will say that I always had my ass in bed as a matter of fact a good friend told me that when I died to request that they bury me face down to give my ass a rest!!! But it all comes back for me, when he told me that

I knew that I wanted to get to a place where I could sleep and not be worried about whatever I had done I wanted to be worry free.. I sleep about four hours a day now and I get a little nap on Saturday afternoon but for all intents and purpose that is it. I will tell you that when I do sleep, I am rested and fine because I have been through my ordeal I can sleep better and with time I am sure that my sleep will get better and longer. I however am a light sleeper and that is no one's fault.

I have not slept well in a long time and I know the reason for most of it. I have been derelict in my duties to God. I mean I say the right things but I have not always done the right things. I have flaws and they do not allow for me to be peaceful. That is a big relief from my shoulders because for so long I have tried to act as if I was above the fray and in control of my situation. If I am a child of God as I profess I need to leave my issues with Him and not just call upon Him when my crack is in a crack. That is why I knew that I was going to prison, I did not listen. I thank God now and more than ever because for so long I have been frustrated and angry, I masked it well because another could not tell how angry I really was, the thoughts I had of hurting someone or having someone hurt that person, one would never know the thoughts that I have had. All because I walked away from what I was supposed to do, I am so glad that grace abounds, because while I still have some anger, I am thankful that it is not what it was and the resulting anger decreases every day. God has truly set me free.

I had a dream some years ago to help others and I did not do what I could have to the extent that I could have and it's bothered me because the difference I could have made would have helped others but I did not. I think in some way we all get what we deserve, when we get it we may not want it the way we are getting it but that's a part of life. So it's somewhat disdainful for me to write this book and say how wrong I was treated when nothing I have done or not done has risen to this level but my efforts to help sure could have been more concentrated instead of what they were. For his reason I am glad that God fiercely pursues those who he loves.

See for so long I had everything a person could want and I had favor pretty much wherever I stepped my foot. Man it's hard to let all that go and I lost it all, not some but all. Paul and prison were my own personal Katrina's. God saved me so that he could continue the work in me and I am so thankful that He did. I am thankful that trouble does not last always, I am thankful that Daniel was in the lion's den, thankful for Joseph being in the well, thankful that Jonah was in the belly of the whale, I am so very thankful that the Sheppard will leave 99 sheep to go and find the one lost sheep. I have been thankful for the story of the sheep being in the well and the workers could not pull it out instead them through dirt on it and with every heaping of dirt the sheep shook it off and rose higher. See the thing that has been opened to my limited vision is to fear not, so when I was imprisoned it was not by man it was God, God freed me in His time and His way, he had to do something to get my attention, because I was not listening. I had it made working in His vineyard but I left every time for the next best thing, when in fact I was toiling for the BEST thing.

So when man thought he put me in jail for whatever the reason, he did not God allowed it just like HE allowed the devil to bother Job, and in that time that I was imprisoned, He walked with me, He talked with me and he told me that I was His, moreover, he told me to fear not. I now know that God allowed these people along the way to play a part in His plan. I for a long time had anger and was frustrated about my situation, I was upset with the government employee's and the devil minions they turned out to be but I realize that God, he had to prepare me for the lesson he had been wanting to teach me. Sure we had some issues along the way and mother has not recovered from the issues she is dealing with but God is still in the plan and He has given a purpose. When you don't listen you leave yourself open to others taking on your responsibility, and one of mine was my child. I have felt bad because by not doing what I have been called to do I have caused someone to raise my child for the time that I was absent. I ask many people not to let this happen to them, please don't make someone else make you mind; don't let someone else take your responsibility and have to treat it as their own.

Can you imagine the frustration of knowing to do something and having the skills and talents to accomplish it and yet not getting it done. I remember watching an advanced aged George Foreman fighting Tommy Morrison in a boxing match. I saw him repeatedly loading up with the punch but not being able to perform and get it dome he got frustrated. I can sympathize with him, because I could do it but did not and it was frustrating. God had to send me on a journey to find out what was important and let me know that I still had work to do. So I am beyond glad that he did not set me up for a comeback, he got my attention to do what I have been told to what to do.

I am closing this short journey with a short story. When I was a sophomore in college I did a term paper on recidivism, I did not know what it was, I had just heard the word on the news and the word really captured me. I did a lot of research on the topic and wrote a very good paper. Some 30 years later without a thought of that term paper written some years ago, I wrote my dissertation on the topic, "recidivism". Of course I was feeling the effects of what had happened to me and was a bit sensitive to the issue, but I never thought of the first paper I turned into professor Dr. Manly Johnson never thought about it. I got word while I was in prison and my dissertation was accepted and thought to be a defining paper. It is interesting how God works through the times and places. Interesting how He will lead you to a point that you think you cannot make it back from and allow you to exceed your talent, but when calls you to action he provides direction not and allows distraction. See no matter the time because he has told us that his time is not our time and that He does not think like we think, when he calls you to service he is going to get the desired service from the desired servant. I am so glad that He was patient with me and surrounded me with patient people because it's not been easy but the road was not meant to be easy, many are called but the chosen are few. I can tell you with certainty and clarity of heart and mind that I know I am a child of God and he loves me. He has pursued me for years and allowed me to slip my hands into the cookie jar, but he saved me and did something that I could not have done on my own, caused the fear to be deleted from my life.

Thank you, God

Ps At the end of all of this, the pre indictment, the indictment, the case in court, Texarkana camp, supervised release and the El Reno imprisonment, after all the heart ache, tears, frustration after all the incredible issues that came along with this case, the illnesses, the tragedies, the lack that my family went through, the loss of employment that really would have set me up for repair and reentry into the world I have become accustomed to, after the toil on my family I want you to know that regarding the judgment for the initial alleged crime which started out at $134,843.31 and is joint and several(which means that the co defendant is to be equally responsible for this debt) . I can say that any payments that have been made have all come from me I am told that I should pay this debt off and sue the co defendant, how nice. The current balance is $127,988.40 which is what they call restitution. After putting me in jail for not paying or so that is what I was told, they have now put me on payments of $100.00 per month and revisit the amount every year. The thing is, I was paying more than this before I went to prison and offered to pay much more then this had they allowed me to work, because they said they sent me to jail for not paying..

EPILOGUE

The Prejudice of Probation

I am Jacques Weston. In 2009, I was sentenced to eighteen months in federal prison and a five-year supervisory release period. I did my time at FCI Texarkana, which was an eye-opening learning experience. Nothing was particularly scary about the place or anything happening within its walls, but I am not saying that I want to spend another moment there either.

My Release to Probation

After serving ten months, I was released to community custody to a halfway house called Wings of Faith. Within the first two weeks there, I asked if I could return to prison to finish my sentence, but my family asked me to rescind the request, so I did. I was sent to the county to complete my halfway house requirement, and I have to tell you: county was the best.

Upon my release on a Monday morning, I went straight to probation. You have up to five days to report for probation, but I wanted to go right away. When I got there, the probation officer, who had also been my pretrial officer, was not pleased to see me. Apparently, I had disturbed his meeting, and I was now officially on his shit list. I took it in jest because we had been cool during pretrial, and I told him he was on mine as well—biggest mistake of my life.

We went through the normal process of probation: I would go in when called; he would come to my house without notice. I had to report within the first five days of the month, and It was always said that the ones who did something wrong would report on that fifth day because they knew they were going to jail. On the first day of every month, I was standing outside waiting for him to get there, rain or shine. I was not going to do anything wrong to jeopardize my situation.

Seeking Employment with a Conviction

I had gotten a hernia in prison and did not have money or insurance to get it fixed, so I was on disability for several months—nothing that I was getting paid for, just disability in terms of working. I was still looking for employment since I could still work, but I just couldn't lift ten pounds, according to the doctor. This greatly impacted the kinds of jobs that I could obtain, but, nonetheless, I went everywhere I could and applied for jobs.

I thought that I had a great chance with the restaurant Cracker Barrel because they needed a nighttime clean-up person. I filled out the application and took it to the restaurant. The manager gave me a spot interview and, during the course of the interview, told me that she liked everything on my application so far. She even asked about my shirt size, if transportation would be a problem—I told her no, as I lived right down the street—hourly wage, and when I could start. Then, she got to the last page of the application and saw that I had checked the box about being to prison. She promptly told me that she had been on vacation the past three weeks and the position had been filled but wished me good luck.

Living in a resort town where gambling and eating are the main attractions would prove to be difficult, to say the last—made more so by the need to secure employment. It was tough for me because I had been a minister before my conviction, and the judge did not allow me to work in the ministry or be self-employed. For many of the positions I applied for, I was told I was overqualified. So, the probation officer had me to go to a call center and swore that I would be able to get a job there. I called the human resources person, and she told me to fill out an application. I did so, but she told me that due to the nature of my conviction, the company that they had the contract with would not allow an employee with a felony record. I plead guilty to one single count of filing a false financial document—that's it, nothing more. The probation officer swore up and down that I was lying and took me to court because he insisted I did not follow his requests. The human resources officer made the statement that I had, in fact, filled out the application but that she could not hire me because of the nature of my felony. The prejudice of probation.

The probation officer would also come by my house when he knew I was not at home. He knew my son played basketball for both the school team and the church league, and he would come by when I was at a game or practice with my son. One of the points of probation is to help the person integrate back into his family, if he still had one when he was released. Yet he constantly cursed at me for spending too much time with my eleven-year-old son. My son, at one point, had to take a cab to school since my mother had wrecked my car when I was at camp. Probation called the school and asked if they knew my son was taking a cab to school. They told him no. He called me and told me I was lying about him taking a cab to school and he was going to come and violate me for lying. He never did, as a mere call to the cab company and a receipt proved differently.

When I was about three-and-a-half years into my five-year term, I went to my monthly beatdown with probation. We were not getting along very well at this point, but no one seems to care about that—or they did not seem to care in my case. At this time, I was still getting there on the first day possible, still getting there by 8 a.m., but now he would let other people filter into the room and see them first. Often, he would wait until 8:50 a.m. to let me into the office, grill me until 9:30 a.m., and smile at me sinisterly, saying, "Oh, you missed your bus and will have to wait an hour for the next bus."

At any rate, on this particular day, he pulled out an application for the racetrack at Oaklawn Racing Casino Resort and pushed it toward me. I told him that I had been to Oaklawn, but they could not hire me in the office because of my felony. He quickly retorted, "I don't want you in the office. I want your Black ass shoveling shit, working where the rest of you no-good niggers belong." His attitude toward me was something the system gets you used to. It's not right, but it is what it is.

At three years and eight months into my five years of supervision, we were still not getting along, but his visits to my house intensified. He often came in and would immediately point to my bedroom, commanding me there, where he would go off on me and say that I was useless and that, if he felt like it, he could make me get on my knees and break it down. What an idiot. I knew that my problem going in was that I gave him too much respect, but over time, my giving of respect eroded greatly. He felt it and always had to maintain the upper hand.

Later, I was working at Crossmark, giving out samples and doing merchandising. Even working twenty-eight hours a week, I was still looking for more, so and he sent me to an employment counselor. She ended up hiring me, so I was then working forty-eight hours a week. The tragic thing is that my release papers called for me to work a full-time job, so even though I was working full-time hours, it was not one job but three. Of course, he complained, filed violation papers, and took me to court.

Me versus Probation: My Second Stay

I was served the papers on my birthday in April. I was due to be off probation by that September. Keep in mind that I had broken no laws, I was paying my fees and fines, working three jobs, and taking care of my family, and I had violated no conditions of supervised release.

To summarize the story, my supervisor at Crossmark would often try to get me more hours by getting the OK for me to work at different stores in Arkansas. On this particular Friday, I was driving up to Ft. Smith to work for the weekend. Ft. Smith, Arkansas, is within my jurisdiction, so I can go there freely without permission. But my supervisor asked for permission anyway, and it was given. Having never been there before, I drove through Little Rock, Arkansas, and got gas before continuing to Ft. Smith. Not a big deal. But, at this time, I was turning my bank statements in to my probation officer. He saw that I had used my debit card to purchase gas in Little Rock, and I told him, yes, I did do that on my way to Ft. Smith. He outlined in my violation papers that I went out of the district without permission. The prejudice of probation.

We went to court, and the judge gave me three conditions to complete:

1. Have surgery
2. Pay restitution on the income tax check I had received
3. Get a full-time job

I was able to do these things in short order, but wouldn't you know it—he sentenced me to nine months in prison anyway. My lawyer asked him, point blank: "Your honor, my client is four-and-a-half years into a five-year supervised release and has not broken any laws, nor has he violated the terms of his release, but you are going to send him to jail for nine months?"

The judge replied, "If you say another word, I will sentence him to three years." My attorney cried in the courtroom. I served the nine difficult months at FCI El Reno. This was a new experience—not scary, but the people were different, and the nine months were hard ones.

The Right to a Fair Trial—for Who?

But that was seven years ago, and, in reflection, nothing about this matter was fair. I call it the prejudice of probation because other offenders of a Caucasian nature were and are treated much better in the system. I was in prison with a Caucasian man who had the same attorney; he stole over $800,000 from his employer and got six months in jail and two years' probation. He had a previous conviction, yet was able to go out of the country during his probation and even got a DUI during his supervision. I know of another person that had served fourteen years in jail for drug possession and dealing. He got two DUI arrests while on probation; the same probation officer got him off early from probation and never violated him for the DUIs or other activities.

I could go on with stories and examples of favorable treatment for my Caucasian brothers. I have a guy right now who was the number-two man in a twenty-three person indictment for drugs. He served two years and had a three-year supervised release, but he has failed three drug tests on three occasions. So what happened to him? They moved him to a different office and got him off supervised release within fifteen months.

The strange thing is that I have seen others do far worse and get off probation early. I have seen guys who served ten years for drugs get out, blow dirty on a drug test not once but twice, and still get off probation early. One guy I know went to jail for drug distribution, got out and blew dirty in Hot Springs, so they moved him out of Hot Springs. He blew dirty at his new probation office, then blew dirty a third time, and he still got off probation three years early. But I also knew a Black guy who had been in jail for dealing drugs but had gotten out. He was in the car with another guy who had drugs in the car. They tested the guy; he came back clean. They did not even arrest the guy I knew, yet probation violated him and sent him back to prison for five years.

I plead guilty to one count of filing a false financial document; the restitution was $134,000, joint and several (meaning two people owe the debt). I got eighteen months and a five-year probationary term. I never broke one law during that time or any violations of my release, yet I got sent back to prison four years and seven months into a five-year supervised release period.

The interesting thing about all of this is that I have since worked to achieve everything that I tried to do while I was on probation. I have obtained my PhD and finished with honors, I have been recognized not once but for five years in a row for my excellence by a national company, and I have my own counseling company. I see forty clients a week, and my company is very successful. The goal of probation is to monitor you and help you reintegrate into society while keeping your family together. I have to tell you: this is only the case for our Caucasian brothers. Prejudice exists in every facet of the alleged justice system. From the jobs given to the rooms assigned and even to the seats in the TV room, prejudice exists.

Some Thoughts on Justice

I reflect on the past a lot, and I honestly believe I have turned the third corner on the lap of completion. Before I finish, I want to share some thoughts.

First, the justice system is anything but just. I was at a federal camp twice for a total of twenty months, and I can tell you for a fact that the sentencing for brown and Black people is totally unfair. I can tell you that the experience of being inside is different for brown and Black people than it is for our white brothers.

Apartheid practiced a policy called relocation, where the people in charge would uproot a Black family so they did not grow deep roots, resulting in family not knowing each other. I will tell you that the US justice system utilizes this system today; they do so by putting Blacks in jail and separating families—sad but true.

Camp was one of the most dehumanizing experiences that someone can withstand. You have the administrative staff, who are basically happy to have a job. I remember a captain at El Reno bullied a citizen because his son had gotten into an incident with another citizen. The captain at the prison ended up being fatally shot because I guess he forgot he was not at the camp. Another guard's wife passed away, and in his sadness, he told the work detail that they were humans just as he was and deserved to be treated fairly. Up until that time, he was a real SOB. Another time, the staff took away the cords to the televisions and did not allow chairs in the television room. When asked about it, the head guard told me that they liked to keep things interesting at the camp. You take the cords to the television so no one could watch and don't allow chairs in the room when most guys depended on the television to break the boredom.

Am I Evil?

I have been sentenced twice in my life: once for my initial court appearance, eighteen months in a camp for the charge of filing a false financial document that they knew I had nothing to do with—as the FBI stated, "We investigated Rev. Weston for two years with a fine-tooth comb and we found nothing against him." Yet, the judge saw fit to call me an evil man. He told my mother that she reminded him of an old Austrian hymn where mothers see their children with rose glasses. What a terrible thing to say to someone's mother. My problem is that I don't consider myself evil, and neither did the three governors, two senators, five congressmen, and the attorneys, doctors and various other people who wrote letters on my behalf.

The second judge who sentenced me was a real joke, sentencing me to nine months on a probation violation when I had broken no laws and broken no violations set forth by the judgment and commitment. I was given nine months because the judge's little playmate, the probation officer, and I did not get along. Yet my attorney openly asked the judge, "Judge, are you really going to give my client nine months when he is four-and-a-half years into a five-year supervised release and has not broken any laws nor has even gotten as much as a traffic ticket?"

The joke—I mean, judge—said, "If you say another word, I will sentence him to three years." In retrospect, he would have had the sentence reversed on appeal because I had broken no laws.

In both matters, the judge felt the need to call me evil. If evil was working forty-eight hours a week, taking care of his family, taking care of his cancer-ridden mother, volunteering at the hospital and donating to charity, then yes, I am evil.

Each time you go before the court, you are asked if you would like to address the court. Each time, both of my attorneys told me not to say anything because it would just piss the judge off. I have often wondered how, exactly, that would piss him off. Neither ever answered my question.

I received the filing a false financial document charge because my "partner" sent said documents to the bank by FedEx. One day while I was at the bank, about to go to lunch with the manager, I asked him to see the file because I wanted to see the documents on which they made the loan. When we were going to lunch the next week, he gave me a copy. I looked through the papers that night and told him the next day that those documents were wrong. The numbers had been greatly inflated, and I mean *greatly* inflated. An evil man does not tell on himself.

I must tell you that the bank is no longer in business. The founder/president had to step down, seeing as he was using the bank as his own wallet. One of its vice presidents was forming companies and making loans to them. She was running her own Ponzi scheme right from the bank. The loss from her was over one million dollars, and she even gave herself a mortgage on a house in one of the better sections of town, bought new cars and jewelry and the finest clothes. She got a tap on the wrist for her actions. After all, it's such stress not to live like the other family members do and it's understandable that she would lie to fit in. Her sentence was nowhere near comparable to my sentence of eighteen months for a restitution of $134,780 that is joint and several—yet I am evil. I know for a fact the judge did not call her evil and even expressed sorrow for the sentence.

It Stays with You

See, my problem is that I can't even drive past the racetrack without hearing the probation officer telling me he wanted me to work at the track—and why. I told him I had been there for a job, but because I was charged with a financial crime, I could not work there. But he had other ideas: he wanted me out in the inclement weather shoveling shit, for that is where I belonged.

I can't drive by the mall and see Sears, which is now out of business, without thinking that they were offering me a job until probation went there and introduced himself, telling them I was stealing from them and not to hire me.

I can't go to my PO box without remembering seeing probation in the back room, undoubtedly going through my mail and opening letters.

I can't drive by my favorite doughnut shop without thinking of the employment agency next door where he sent me to look for work. In his violation report, he claimed that I lied about going there when he told me to.

But I had gone. Once again, because of the nature of the contract, I could not work in the call center, so the head of human resources told me not to fill out an application. When it was brought up in court, the emailed statement from the human resources staff was quickly made moot.

These things I could deal with if the field of play was level, but it was not. The system of justice is rigged. It's geared toward those that the people in power resemble or can identify with because they understand them. None of the tenements or principles set forth by the justice department for felons coming home have ever been fair for brown and Black people.

I remember my eldest brother, Danny, with a great deal of fondness and love. But something he used to do to me growing up reared its head in my probation meetings. Danny would walk up to me, and when he got close, he would buck his eyes, and I always knew a punch or a slap was coming. Somehow, probation knew. Whether it was written somewhere deep in my file or whether someone did an interview with someone who knew me and told probation, it didn't matter. He knew that this bothered the hell out of me, but for two to three years, I would go to probation office for the monthly beatdown, and he would proceed to buck his eyes. Now, the first couple of times that he did it, I was transported back to my brother, but as time went on, it became very agitating, *very* agitating. I truly believe that he enjoyed performing this beatdown. By the end of my probation, someone had to sit in the office with us and the door had to be kept open. It's one thing to respect your job; it's another thing to use the position to become an irritant. This guy is one of the few people I have been around that I have absolutely no respect or concern for. I forgive him and pray for him, but I have nothing left for him.